THE
CHAMPIONSHIPS
WIMBLEDON

Official Annual 1988

JOHN PARSONS
Photographs by TOMMY HINDLEY

AURUM PRESS

Photographs copyright © Tommy Hindley 1988; additional
photographs by Professional Sports photographic team of
Chris Cole, Philip Shephard-Lewis, Matthew Risby and Jim
Steele.
The photograph on p.5 is copyright © Universal Pictorial
Press and Agency Ltd; on pp. 10-11 © Aerofilms Ltd.

First published 1988 by Aurum Press Ltd, 33 Museum
Street, London WC1A 1LD

All photographs were taken on Kodak Professional film.

ISBN 0 948149 99 X

Typeset by Bookworm Typesetting, Manchester
Printed and bound in Great Britain by
Butler and Tanner Ltd, Frome

FOREWORD

This is the sixth Wimbledon Annual, telling the story of our 1988 Championship Meeting. What a pity that every year since 1877 has not been similarly commemorated.

Nevertheless, as a record in words and pictures of the last six Meetings, these annuals are a fascinating reminder, both written and illustrated, of just what happened in the years 1983 to 1988 on the lawns of The All England Lawn Tennis and Croquet Club.

Perhaps this year, after a first week of beautiful weather, we became over-confident, but the nightmare of rain and intermittent showers as we reached the final two days soon brought us back to earth – and pretty damp earth at that. Thank goodness for court covers. Indeed, we only just managed it by 8.45 pm on Monday 4 July, otherwise we would have been forced to open the grounds for yet another day.

Second-week weather apart, it was a happy and rewarding fortnight with some thrilling matches and the emergence of two young and worthy champions in Stefan Edberg of Sweden and Steffi Graf of West Germany. The only title to be successfully defended was the Men's Doubles by Ken Flach and Robert Seguso; the Ladies' Doubles went to an exciting 12–10 in the final set, victory going to Steffi Graf and Gabriela Sabatini; in the Mixed Doubles, Sherwood Stewart and Zina Garrison triumphed, the former getting his name on the Roll of Honour for the first time at the age of 42. His tears of joy were evidence of the esteem in which our great Championships are held.

I will end by congratulating the Committee of Management, the Staff, the Referee and the hundreds of hard-working and willing people who, in spite of all the difficulties, brought our 1988 Meeting to a successful close.

R. E. H. Hadingham, CBE, MC, TD
Chairman of The All England Club and the Committee of Management of The Lawn Tennis Championships

July 1988

INTRODUCTION

Seldom has any Wimbledon in recent years started with so many players having so much at stake or wishing to prove so much as the 1988 Championships. A reasonable case could be made out for any one of at least six of those chasing the men's singles title. Among the women, the relative merits and strengths of Martina Navratilova and Steffi Graf on grass, and especially on Wimbledon's grass, fuelled as lively a debate as ever.

On top of the normal considerations of form, fitness and that special fortitude needed to sustain the highest standards throughout a Wimbledon fortnight, there were additional factors to be taken into consideration, not least, in the men's singles, that John McEnroe was back.

In common-sense deference to his playing record at Wimbledon in recent years, the seeding committee lifted him to eighth place on their list, six rungs higher than he would have been on a ladder solely reflecting the latest world rankings.

Could the three times former champion find both the stamina and strength of will, after two years away from The Championships and much of the previous 10 months away from competitive tennis altogether, to reproduce those wondrously gifted skills which used to lift his lawn tennis into a jewelled class of its own? He and a growing number of converts during the days leading up to Wimbledon thought he could.

Just as many, however, were equally convinced that Pat Cash, despite having won only one title on the Nabisco Grand Prix since conquering the game's own Everest in 1987, could successfully defend the trophy. Or that Boris Becker could show that his second round defeat a year earlier was nothing more than 'one of those things' and resume what many felt might become a Bjorn Borg-style tradition, after his victory not only in 1985, at the age of 17 to become Wimbledon's youngest men's singles champion, but again in 1986.

Then there was world champion Ivan Lendl. Surely it would be his turn sooner or later. And of course there were also the Swedes – Mats Wilander, already halfway to the Grand Slam as winner of the Australian and French titles, and Stefan Edberg who, as usual, had been content to remain in relative obscurity while quietly but astutely directing his preparations during 1988 towards one target: Wimbledon.

It takes far more than omens or lucky coincidences to win Wimbledon, but if Edberg had been looking for one, it was available. When he won the junior boys' singles at Wimbledon in 1983 the player he succeeded to the title was Pat Cash. Coincidences do sometimes happen.

Everything in the women's singles, of course, was focused on whether Martina Navratilova, unbeaten since the semi-finals of 1981, could become the champion for a record ninth time; or would Steffi Graf, one year older and wiser than the last time she tried to break the American's dominance at Wimbledon, spoil the party?

There was no doubting what Miss Navratilova felt about the approaching fortnight. In a moment of quiet reflection in Paris a few weeks earlier she said, 'Winning Wimbledon always was and always will be everything – and I mean everything – in tennis terms. I have always done well there because it is so special. The enjoyment of playing there takes over the pressure.

'If I win the ninth title, I could sit back, enjoy myself, smell the roses and wallow in it. No one could take it away from me. Of all the titles and all the victories, this is the one which is going to mean the most. I know I'll be happy never to play another match if I can win my ninth at Wimbledon.'

Who, other than Miss Graf, who was also halfway to achieving the Grand Slam after winning the Australian and French titles without even conceding a single set, would – or could – have denied her that?

Over the next 15 days, as it so happened, after the weather so cruelly intervened on the final weekend, all these issues would be resolved, bringing with them the usual stories of unbridled joy and abject disappointment. The Wimbledon magic still reigns supreme.

D A Y 1

Monday 20 June

The first round and, especially, the first day of any Grand Slam tournament can often be much more testing for the leading contenders than many might suppose. It is a time for settling back into those adjusted routines of mind and muscle on grass, which the players hope will become instinctive as quickly as possible, and of allowing that special Wimbledon inspiration to filter through to their bones.

On a hot and often sultry day Boris Becker, Pat Cash, Ivan Lendl and Stefan Edberg, who at this stage and in that order were among the most obvious contenders, were well satisfied with their first day's work. Cash, in particular, was swiftly back into that familiar solid serve and volley routine which eventually enabled him to scale such spectacular heights, in more ways than one, the last time he was the focus of such eager attention on the world's most famous court.

Then Lendl, the world champion, was the opponent receiving a grass court lesson. This time it was Todd Woodbridge, 17, one of a growing number of young Australians establishing themselves on the circuit after being initially spurred on, at least in part, by Cash's triumphant example.

Woodbridge, who had sneaked at least a glimpse of the Cash–Lendl final the year before, while waiting to go out to win the boys' doubles, had earned his place in the draw this year the hard way – as a qualifier. No doubt much more will be heard of him in the future but, at this stage of his development, he was very much the servant to the master as Cash, without any hint of sentiment or sympathy, beat him 6–1, 6–2, 6–2. 'It's pretty good to be back and it's a very nice court. It didn't feel as if I'd been off it,' said Cash after his comfortable, contented progress against a junior with a men's ranking of 262.

Lendl, at least publicly, was less impressed by the style of his own 6–4, 6–1, 6–3 defeat of British wild card, David Felgate. Others, including Felgate, who in fact applied himself encouragingly well until Lendl's serve found the right groove and started skidding past him with bewildering regularity, thought the world champion had every reason to be pleased; especially as there was no sign of Lendl being restricted by the pulled pectoral muscle which had meant his defence of the French Open ending much earlier than almost anyone could have anticipated.

Lendl in fact hit 20 aces against Felgate, including one on each of the occasions when Felgate held a break point against him; one more to finish the first set, four in the fourth game of the second set and then three in a row in the fifth game of the third set.

Becker also hit 20 aces, including one to win each of his first five service games, as he went through 6–3, 6–1, 6–2 against John Frawley, the Australian whose brother, Rod, was an unseeded semi-finalist in 1981. Towards the end of a match which did not finish until 8.58 pm Becker had considerable problems with his footing, although in a match which he knew he was always going to win it did not bother him unduly. Twice he won points while lying flat on his back. On several other occasions he showed that he was as enthusiastic and adept as ever at diving full length in search of winners.

After one fierce forehand which went astray and struck the net cord judge, Rachel Boley, in the ribs, he could not resist the opportunity, much to the crowd's amusement and the embarrassment of the blushing official, to run up and help her rub the injury better. No one seemed to mind, but later in The Championships some of Becker's playful diversions were not seen in quite the same light.

Ironically, in view of future events, the only leading seed to drop a set on the opening Monday was Edberg. Nevertheless he generally seemed to be relaxed and in overall control of his

A typical view of Boris Becker in confident mood as he beat John Frawley.

game, as he beat the fierce-serving Frenchman, Guy Forget, 6–4, 3–6, 6–3, 6–4. Edberg had also defeated the left-hander in the semi-finals at Queen's Club, ten days earlier, immediately before losing to Becker in the final. The erratic serving, which had denied him the dominance at the net necessary on that occasion, seemed to be a thing of the past.

Edberg had just broken for 2–1 in the fourth set when, to the accompaniment of rolling thunder, play was delayed for 45 minutes. Psychologically it was not a bad moment to have made the breakthrough. On the resumption of play, it was all over in a further 20 minutes. One outcome of the rain was that the Jimmy Connors match with Leif Shiras was postponed and Connors was not the only former champion who had an unexpected extra day's preparation.

Whatever initial disappointment that day's

It was probably too much to hope for a first day without at least one brief interruption by rain.

Court 1 crowd may have felt at not being able to welcome John McEnroe back to Wimbledon for the first time since 1985 (his opponent, Austria's Horst Skoff, had won the Athens Grand Prix title only the day before) was increasingly dispelled as Jeremy Bates, although unconvincing early on, provided them with a rare British treat.

The still-packed crowd was naturally as jubilant as the British number one himself as he produced a magnificent comeback, not only from two sets down but also from 0–3 in the third, at the end of an otherwise almost wholly predictable first day.

The player on the receiving end of much whirlwind serving and returning by Bates was Christo Van Rensburg, ranked 36, from South Africa, who only four days earlier had beaten McEnroe. 'Although I've won matches over five sets before, that's the first time I've done so from two sets down,' said Bates, who never looked back after breaking his opponent's serve for the first time in the fourth game of the third set, and went on to win 2–6, 1–6, 6–3, 7–5, 6–4.

Christo Van Rensburg lost a two sets lead against Jeremy Bates.

British cheers for Stephen Botfield, as he upset Czechoslovakia's Jaro Navratil.

Van Rensburg's serve, it has to be said, proved vulnerable, almost to the point of reckless generosity. There were 13 double faults, including three as Bates broke crucially for 6–5 in the fourth set and then just had time, amid worsening drizzle, to make it two sets all before they were forced off court for 90 minutes.

Bates was not alone in raising British cheers. Earlier on Court 4, Stephen Botfield, who had achieved fleeting recognition two years before by defeating Emilio Sanchez in the first round, when the Spaniard was the 16th seed, upset the rankings with a 6–4, 6–4, 6–3 victory over Czechoslovakian Jaro Navratil. Botfield was ranked 442, his opponent 137. At that level it was essentially the difference between one player who was happy to play on grass and another who was apprehensive.

'It's easy to play well here,' commented Botfield, not meaning it to sound arrogant in any way. 'I look forward to Wimbledon every year. This is where I want to win most. If you don't want to win at Wimbledon then you don't want to win anywhere.'

Elsewhere, however, there were all too many examples of British players, if not exactly showing the white flag, failing to prevent expected losses. Stephen Shaw took the third set from Wally Masur, whose real moment of glory was still to come; Nick Fulwood took the second of four sets from Greg Holmes; and Mark Petchey,

No luck in the draw for the Sanchez brothers.

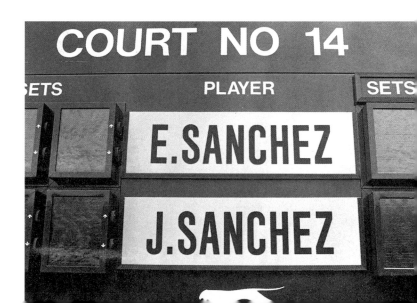

Jeremy Bates (above) staged the finest comeback of his career against Christo Van Rensburg.

Emilio Sanchez (left) kept younger brother Javier in his place – again.

Michael Chang, at 16 the youngest winner of a men's singles match at Wimbledon since 1911.

Pat Cash begins the defence of his title.

the Essex schoolboy who had taken a history A-level paper that morning, showed promise as Britain's top junior before losing 6–3, 7–5, 6–4 to West Germany's Heiner Moraing.

An abrupt, almost chilling reminder of the gulf between British standards and those in so many other parts of the world, however, came when Michael Chang, the outstanding young American prospect, beat American qualifier Glenn Layendecker 7–5, 1–6, 6–4, 6–2 to become the youngest to win a men's singles match at Wimbledon in over 60 years.

In the now traditional limited women's programme on opening day, Australia's Anne Minter had the distinction of becoming the first winner, and France's Pascale Paradis, a former world junior champion, was the first to knock out a seed, although on grass her confident 6–4, 6–3 victory over clay-courter Manuela Maleeva did not create many shockwaves. All three British girls in action lost their matches, Clare Wood most disappointingly from a set and 3–0 up against the American, Robin White.

Finally on this straightforward but none the less exhilarating first day, the clash between the Sanchez brothers, Emilio and Javier, was the first involving brothers in a Grand Slam tournament in Open tennis and the first at Wimbledon for more than half a century. As in all their previous meetings elsewhere, Emilio, this time seeded 13, was the winner. The score was 6–3, 6–3, 6–4.

Left: Anne Minter – the first match winner in 1988.

After taking an A-level exam in the morning, British junior Mark Petchey was on the losing end of his first round test by West Germany's Heiner Moraing.

D A Y

2

Tuesday 21 June

It is customary to refer to the first Tuesday of Wimbledon as 'Ladies' Day'. That was certainly appropriate on this occasion, for although the emphasis on fashion may have diminished, the day was still marked by special celebrations.

Chris Evert, for instance, who first played at Wimbledon in 1972 and went on to win the title three times, stepped out to play her 100th singles match and duly recorded her 87th win when she beat a determined French teenager, Alexia Dechaume, 6–1, 6–2. As a bonus, she also reported that the recurring heel problem which had forced her to default in Rome and led to her defeat by the Spanish teenager, Aranxta Sanchez, in Paris was no longer a cause for primary concern.

Not to be outdone, Martina Navratilova, who, as defending champion, had opened the Centre Court proceedings for the sixth consecutive year, beat Sabrina Goles from Yugoslavia, also 6–1, 6–2, to take her past Bjorn Borg's post-war record of 42 consecutive singles wins. 'I'd put money on me right now,' said Miss Navratilova, 'I'm a heck of a bet (at 13–8).'

Yet both these leading ladies of a dynasty which had dominated women's tennis for well over a decade were outshone by Steffi Graf, who had arrived at Wimbledon with a stronger serve, more effective backhand and certainly more confidence on grass than the previous year, when those three aspects of her game were all

problematic as she lost in the final.

In winning the Australian and the French titles, Miss Graf failed to concede even a set. In the French final she beat Natalia Zvereva, who had upset Miss Navratilova, 6–0, 6–0. Against Miss Na Hu on Wimbledon's Court 1 the score was the same, 6–0, 6–0. Even Miss Graf's father, who is renowned for his superstitious pessimism – at least publicly – about some of her matches, said, 'I've never seen her play so well on grass. If she continues to play like this, she'll have no problems.' It was all over in 46 minutes. Even at this stage Miss Graf, the top seed, was already a shade faster than the only rival most people seemed to think could upset her. Miss Navratilova's match had taken 49 minutes.

With Gabriela Sabatini beating Carling (Bassett) Seguso 6–2, 6–2, of the leading contenders only Pam Shriver, fighting off glandular fever and injuries with pills, glue, sticking plasters and straps, as we were to discover later, really had to struggle in the first round. Miss Shriver, who is never less than whole-hearted in her approach to whatever she is doing, especially (and thankfully) in interviews, was pushed almost to the brink before resisting Dinky Van Rensburg, 6–2, 4–6, 8–6.

In a marathon final set, Miss Van Rensburg led 4–1 with a point for 5–1. At that stage, according to Miss Shriver, the South African was 'serving out of her brain'. At 4–2, however, in striving to place those biting serves too close to the lines, Miss Van Rensburg double-faulted twice to lose the initiative. 'To get to that sort of position and let it slip when, from a career point of view, you need to break through is pretty depressing,' said Miss Van Rensburg, whose only other point on Miss Shriver's serve from 4–3 was a double fault in the final game.

At 5–6 in the third set, Miss Shriver, who missed 11 break points in four games in the second set, glanced across from Court 13 and noticed that the scoreboards on the clubhouse showed that Miss Graf was leading 6–0, 4–0 and Miss Navratilova 6–1, 4–1 in their matches. 'It crosses your mind then that you wish your life was a little easier,' she reflected wistfully.

Steffi Graf – for her, it seems, the sky is the limit.

Pam Shriver, struggling against injury and illness, dropped the second set against Dinky Van Rensburg, but it turned out fine for her in the end.

One down, six matches still to go, as Martina Navratilova sets out in search of a record ninth title.

A promising effort by Richard Whichello before injury handicapped him.

Gabriela Sabatini poised for action.

These visitors clearly let Wimbledon go to their heads.

Jo Durie became the first British woman to win a match, but only after tormenting her followers on Court 1 for more than an hour. That was especially so while a commanding 5–1 lead in the first set was being whittled away, but at least she held her nerve to beat the American, Marianne Werdel, 6–4, 6–2. Sara Gomer also won, late in the evening, 7–6, 6–4 against another American, Penny Barg, while two courts away at 8.50 pm Monique Javer, competing at Wimbledon for the first time under a Union Jack banner, was still battling against West Germany's Silke Meier.

In the end Miss Javer, who had looked impressively in control in the first set, went down 2–6, 6–3, 9–7 and so joined a whole procession of early British losers, in a year when the gulf between the top eight or so in the women's singles and the rest looked wider and more disappointing than ever.

Among the British men, Richard Whichello, 21, enabled by a wild card to play at Wimbledon for the first time, won the first set and was within a tie-break of taking the second before a leg injury contributed to his 5–7, 7–6, 7–5, 6–2 defeat. Much more frustrating for those, not only in Britain, who yearn for the country which founded lawn tennis and which stages its finest tournament to become a credible playing power in the game again, Andrew Castle went out to Canada's Glenn Michibata, 6–4, 7–5, 6–4. Michibata was 50 places below the 91st-ranked Castle, but was always significantly sharper in thought and deed. Three wins in qualifying had once again proved so beneficial.

The major moment of the day, though, was the return of John McEnroe. The prodigal son could hardly have been made to feel more welcome. He was cheered both on to and off Wimbledon's Court 1 where, in his bad old days, boos and jeers echoed in his ears. In between his two rapturous receptions he almost disdainfully brushed aside Horst Skoff, 6–1, 7–5, 6–1, and there was a touch of irony in the fact that for once it was he, rather than his opponent, who became irritated by the attitude of the man on the other side of the net.

Serious business by Mats Wilander, the Australian and French champion, as he launches his Wimbledon bid against Argentina's Eduardo Masso.

Skoff had practised for only 20 minutes on grass and despite some booming serves too often gave the impression that he might as well make it fun while it lasted – which he clearly did not expect to be very long. In fact, with McEnroe hitting a growing ratio of spectacular returns, the third set lasted a mere 24 minutes, including three 90-second change-overs.

As usual McEnroe had plenty to say afterwards, mostly comments people wanted or were interested to hear, not least his call to other Grand Slam tournaments to follow Wimbledon's example in basing their seedings on the record and ability of each player on the surface involved. He called Wimbledon's decision to lift him from 14th position (where those who feel rankings should be sacrosant would have placed him) to eighth in the seedings 'a nice gesture'.

On Centre Court Mats Wilander's backhand was in brilliant form, whether hit two-fisted or single-handed, as he firmly rebuffed Eduardo Masso, 24, a left-handed Argentinian who at times evoked memories of Guillermo Vilas, 6–3, 6–4, 7–6. Masso delayed Wilander's victory by saving a match point at 5–3 in the third set. He broke back with a stupendous backhand stop volley and even led 4–0 in the tie-break before the Australian and French champion took the next seven points.

Jimmy Connors who, like Chris Evert, has been a constant competitor at Wimbledon since 1972, was in typically aggressive, exuberant and impish mood as he efficiently packed off Leif Shiras, 6–3, 7–6, 6–1. Some of the rallies provided vintage entertainment for an overflowing crowd on Court 2. After one particularly hectic exchange of close-in volleys, Shiras forlornly threw his racket at the ball and it finished up on the other side of the net. Connors could not resist the temptation to do the same. Amid the ensuing confusion the ball boys returned the rackets to the wrong owners. For a couple of points the players pretended that they had not noticed.

It was on this court that Connors lost to Kevin Curren in the quarter-finals. This time, while the former champion was registering his 93rd singles victory in The Championships, Curren, who needed his ankle taped at 3–3 in the third set, was losing next door on Court 3 to the Chilean, Ricardo Acuna, a qualifier for the second time in four years. In 1985, as a qualifier, Acuna beat Pat Cash and reached the last eight.

Two seeds, it was thought, could have been in trouble, although as it turned out neither actually was. Jonas Svensson, who had beaten Ivan Lendl in Paris and since been laid low by hay fever, beat Tim Wilkison 6–1, 7–6, 6–3, and Miloslav Mecir, although reluctant to serve full out, successfully came through the test on his back injury which had kept him out of Grand Prix tennis since April, with a 7–6, 7–6, 6–2 defeat of the Mexican, Agustin Moreno.

What a difference a year makes. In 1987 Peter Doohan was the toast of the news reporters for giving them the first off-beat story of the tournament when he beat Boris Becker in the second round. This time only the major tennis writers noticed his first round defeat in straight sets by Ken Flach.

Nor did the two seeds who were eliminated attract the newsmen. The defeat of 14th-seeded Andrei Chesnokov by Udo Riglewski, 21, the 13th-ranked West German with a world ranking of 127, and the withdrawal of Claudia Kohde-Kilsch through injury, meant nothing to them on the day 'Mac was back'.

Andrew Castle, often his own biggest critic, as he lost in the first round to Canadian Glenn Michibata.

'Nothing seems to have changed' appears to be the thought going through John McEnroe's mind, as he beats Horst Skoff from Austria.

D A Y 3

Wednesday 22 June

Day three dawned warm and sunny. Nearly 37,000 passed through the gates of The All England Club but the combination of the additional seats on Courts 14 and 17 and the new walkway on the west side of Court 1 helped to make sure there was little of the uncomfortable crowding experienced on corresponding days in previous years.

What pressure there was mainly centred upon defending champion Pat Cash. It was only in the nick of time that he suddenly managed to lift what for a while was a surprisingly ragged, faltering game to avoid the same sort of second round catastrophe which befell his predecessor, Boris Becker, a year earlier.

On the same Court 1 where Becker yielded his crown to Peter Doohan in a manner he will never be able to explain satisfactorily to himself, Cash had to fight back from two sets to one down to beat the Argentinian, Javier Frana, 6–2, 4–6, 3–6, 6–1, 6–4.

'I'm happy with the way I played for three sets. In the other two he just played too well,' said Cash, indicating that his main problem had been that the court was 'soft and not even. It's been chewed up in the middle and there it's a mess.'

That was an altogether too simple explanation, however, for the enormous difficulties he encountered against a lively, quick-learning left-hander who had taken only two games from

Cash a fortnight earlier at Queen's Club. Then he was the one who slipped all over the court. This time it was Cash who frequently stumbled or skidded before pulling things into shape in the last two sets.

Frana, who was quick to punish Cash for unforced errors and for not putting his volleys and overheads away with the same venom he demonstrated in 1987, said that after the third set he really thought he could win. Had it not been for a controversial point which helped Cash break for 3–1 in the fourth set, it might have become very interesting indeed. 'The next match I'll get there,' insisted Cash, but somehow he did not seem as confident about that, either, as one would have expected.

By coincidence neither Becker nor Lendl looked as comfortable as in their first matches. The 1985 and 1986 champion, still five months away from his 21st birthday, hit 17 aces against Karel Novacek and never allowed the Czechoslovakian a break point while registering a 6–3, 6–4, 6–4 victory.

'It wasn't easy to play on Court 2,' Becker said, citing the noise (most of it from the players' balcony) and 'many people moving around'. No doubt his memory of how, on his first Wimbledon visit in 1984, he was helped away from this court in a wheelchair after twisting his ankle against Bill Scanlon added to his discomfort. To some extent Becker's short journeys to and from the dressing rooms through a screaming avenue of young fans, prompting comparison with the days of Borgomania, caused him just as many problems as the match, in which Novacek earned one game more than on their previous encounter, when they opened the 1987 Centre Court programme.

In another match which demonstrated his uncertainty and therefore his potential frailty on grass, Lendl dropped the first set before imposing his heavier serving and ability to come up with big shots on the biggest points, to beat Australian Darren Cahill, 5–7, 6–2, 6–4, 6–4.

Apart from the final game of a stimulating opening set, when Cahill broke him with a blazing backhand down the line, Lendl was generally in control. He adjusted his game to

Boris Becker being escorted back to the dressing rooms amid his admiring fans, after beating Karel Novacek.

A tough time for Pat Cash before he completed a happy second round landing against Javier Frana.

'Well done!' Henri Leconte congratulates American Michael Chang, after resisting his fighting challenge on Centre Court in the second round.

cope more effectively with Cahill's serve and remarked, 'My play seems to be more solid this year than last year at the same time. The more you play on grass, the more comfortable you feel.'

Cahill chipped in to boost Lendl's morale still further by saying, 'If he serves like that throughout the whole tournament, he has a very good chance, along with five or six other guys.' Cahill went on to list them but, like most people at that stage, there was one Swedish name he significantly overlooked.

There was no doubt about the match of the day. That came, as so often seems to be the case, late in the evening on Centre Court when Henri Leconte, the Frenchman already well established as a favourite with the crowds, survived an electrifying challenge from Michael Chang, 16, the diminutive Californian who earned himself an instant fan club.

Chang, already high enough in the world rankings to have been accepted straight into the draw on merit, showed exactly why the Americans believe they have found a potential new major challenger for the first time since John McEnroe, before running out of energy after four marvellously competitive and richly entertaining sets.

When it was over Leconte, who had won 2–6, 7–6, 6–2, 6–3, jumped the net and put his arm round the teenager, clapping his racket to lead the applause for Chang. The near-capacity crowd, which had responded excitedly to endless stinging and spectacular double-fisted passing shots and volleys, maintained their ovation for a full two minutes until the players left the court.

Leconte described the way in which Chang applied himself to his task and the tennis he produced in the first two sets as 'unbelievable', adding, 'I've never seen anyone return my serve for two sets like that. He was all over the place, hitting winners on both flanks, and he's so fast. He also has a good mentality. He just came out with the feeling that he had nothing to lose. In a few years, when there's more pressure on him, it will be different, and for sure he has to improve his serve.'

Time will show us if that is the case. At this stage, however, Chang greatly impressed as a prospect with huge promise, and certainly he played his full part in providing Wimbledon with one of those emotional clashes in the late

Being a ball boy can be thirsty work.

evening sunshine which deserve to be remembered as far more than just another second round match.

The day had begun with the early departure of 15th-seeded Amos Mansdorf from Israel – mainly because, when trailing 3–6, 0–3, he could no longer battle on against Diego Nargiso, an Italian qualifier, because of a pulled stomach muscle.

At the start of the fortnight there had been 25 players from the United States and 13 from Sweden in the draw. By the end of the first round 15 Americans and 10 Swedes remained, but then the Swedes found themselves having to knock one another out. That was the case as Joakim Nystrom beat Jan Gunnarsson and Jonas Svensson removed Magnus Gustafsson.

In the women's singles day three was uplifted, if that is the correct term, by the match in which Barbara Potter decided to change her shirt on court in a marathon struggle before she overcame Natalia Bykova, one of five Russian players taking part in the women's singles, 2–6, 6–4, 9–7. Miss Bykova took a 3–0 lead in the second set before Miss Potter, with a world ranking of 18, managed to pull her game round.

The American, who has three times been a Wimbledon quarter-finalist, had the words 'Smart Arse' emblazoned on another intimate part of her apparel which she did not change. The words nearly rebounded on her.

Meanwhile two British girls, playing well above their rankings and international reputations but not, one hopes, their ultimate potential, provided the two relative surprises of the day. Sarah Loosemore, 17, the Welsh schoolgirl playing her first Wimbledon, and Julie Salmon, 22, from Brighton, provided some delight on the outside courts with their almost simultaneous victories over the vastly more experienced Peanut Louie Harper and former women's doubles champion, Liz Smylie.

Just as Miss Salmon was punching the air to celebrate a 6–4, 6–4 victory over the Australian who had beaten her at Edgbaston two weeks earlier, Miss Loosemore was serving for her 6–7, 6–3, 6–4 first round defeat of Mrs Harper, an American ranked 150 places above her.

The French girl, Karine Quentrec, 17, who had come in as a lucky loser from qualifying to replace the injured Rafaella Reggi and had then beaten her French junior compatriot, Julie Halard, was nearly late for her token appearance against Steffi Graf. She had been engrossed in watching Pascale Paradis save six match points against her doubles partner before beating Nathalie Herreman 6–4, 3–6, 8–6 in another all-French tussle.

Miss Graf, who warmed up while she was waiting by playing shots with a ball girl, much to the crowd's delight and amusement, took a mere 35 minutes to reach a 6–2, 6–0 victory.

Patience is a virtue – even in a journalist.

A solid win for Britain's Julie Salmon over the more experienced Australian, Liz Smylie.

Steffi Graf gave an excited ball girl a few hints while waiting for her real opponent to arrive.

*Barbara Potter found the going painful before she
overcame Russia's Natalia Bykova.*

D A Y 4

Thursday 23 June

John McEnroe was not alone in thinking that he was ready to make at least a realistic bid to regain the Wimbledon crown he last wore in 1984. In particular the two brilliant sets he played against Ivan Lendl in Paris had convinced friend and foe alike that the old magical touch and control were returning in sufficient depth.

We were all wrong. At 8.04 pm, on a Centre Court buzzing with excitement and much disbelief, McEnroe was knocked out in the second round, 7–5, 7–6, 6–3, by the Australian Wally Masur. Eighteen months earlier, in Melbourne, Masur had beaten Boris Becker in a manner which persuaded the then Wimbledon champion's coach, Gunther Bosch, to part company with the West German.

'If that's the best I have to give, I'd quit tomorrow,' said eighth-seeded McEnroe, who drifted into a severe bout of self-recrimination after realizing that his tennis was but a shadow of the glorious, probably unrivalled skills which graced these Championships, between some tantrums, a few years ago.

McEnroe's worst fears were more about preparation, strength and stamina than basic skills, as he suffered his earliest Wimbledon defeat since fellow American Erik van Dillen beat him in the first round of 1978. It was true, he said, 'I couldn't do the basics, and if you can't do that you can't do anything.' Yet that stem-

med from the insufficient build-up, especially on grass, and his lack of real stamina.

The truth was that McEnroe continued to think and talk like the perfectionist he has always been; but he can no longer play like one. The chances were certainly available. He had set points in each of the first two sets and two points to go ahead 4–2 in the third set. On the first he stamped his foot in annoyance after a feeble backhand. On the second Masur's volley was too deep, right on to the baseline, for him to react profitably.

Masur, who throughout had played the ideal game for the occasion, striking his serves heavily and wide, pulling McEnroe out of position, just as the American had done to his opponents so often in the past, then hooked another volley so close to the baseline that the former champion thought it was out. Not for the first time McEnroe bounced his racket on the court in frustration and was given a code violation for racket abuse. To suggest, however, as some of the newspapers did the next morning, that the former bad boy of tennis had thrown another 'tantrum' was untrue and unfair.

After Masur, 23, who was born in Southampton but emigrated to Australia while he was still a babe in arms, almost nervously put away the match-winning forehand volley, McEnroe walked grim-faced to the net to shake his opponent by the hand. 'Masur played a good solid match and I couldn't come up with anything,' he admitted. 'I never felt I was in sync with my game. For me to go out there and play the way I played is embarrassing.'

That was being far too hard on himself. He was much nearer the mark when he went on to say of his comeback, 'I expected some ups and downs and it's not really surprising that something like this should happen. I felt I could win the tournament but I also felt that this could happen. It was just one of those days.'

Two other seeds went out of the men's singles. The 11th-seeded Anders Jarryd, a semi-finalist three years earlier when, but for an overnight break for rain, he might just have prevented Becker from going on to make history as the tournament's youngest champion, was

Glenn Michibata defended athletically, but to no avail, against Mats Wilander on Court 1.

John McEnroe tries to blot out his impending defeat by Wally Masur.

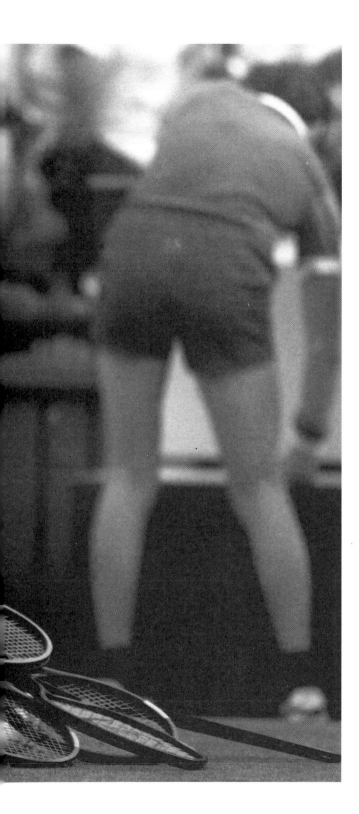

beaten 3–6, 7–6, 6–3, 6–0 by the tall Californian, Jim Grabb. Much of Jarryd's resistance seemed to evaporate after the match went horribly wrong for him from 3–0 in the second set tie-break. Three times before he eventually conceded the tie-break 7–5 he was beaten by shots off the frame. Grabb, one of only eight Americans then left in the competition, compared with 16 at this stage in 1984, swept through almost unopposed from 3–3 in the third set. Jarryd held only five points in the brief fourth set. Emilio Sanchez lost, less surprisingly, to Petr Korda's serving, 7–6, 6–3, 3–6, 0–6, 6–1.

Jimmy Connors, 35, again took pleasure in putting a youngster in his place when he beat Jason Stoltenberg, the Australian who learned his tennis on an anthill court, with chicken wire for a net, on his parents' farm near the quaintly named town of Wee Wa. The score was 7–6, 6–3, 6–3.

Meanwhile, still without attracting undue notice from the bookmakers or their clients, Stefan Edberg beat Richey Reneberg, the American who pushed Ivan Lendl so well the year before, 6–3, 7–6, 5–7, 6–2, in precisely the sort of match a blossoming contender for the title needed at this stage. The way he staved off three points which could have cost him the second set tie-break was the sort of evidence which was never fully recognized until much later.

A measure of Edberg's growing confidence was demonstrated when he was asked to list those whom he thought could win the title. He began very firmly by responding 'Me', before adding 'Cash, Becker, Lendl and Wilander'.

For a man with Grand Slam thoughts starting to develop in his mind, Wilander looked remarkably calm and relaxed on Court 1 where, unperturbed by missing three volleys to lose his serve in the opening game, he went on to dismiss qualifier Glenn Michibata 6–2, 7–6, 6–4. One qualifier who did make further progress, however, was Ricardo Acuna, who saved four match points in the fourth set tie-break on his way to defeating David Pate, 3–6, 5–7, 7–6, 7–6, 6–4, in three hours 42 minutes.

Derrick Rostagno, the Californian, won despite yielding two match points in a third set tie-break, but it took him four hours 45 minutes to put away another American, Marty Davis, 6–2, 6–3, 6–7, 4–6, 16–14.

On the British front, interest in the men's singles was once more all too swiftly a matter of

No prizes for guessing what Jo Durie is saying to herself as another shot against Ros Fairbank missed its target by an inch.

A comfortable win for Helena Sukova over fellow Czechoslovakian Jana Novotna.

history. Stephen Botfield was beaten 6–2, 6–3, 6–4 by the more experienced Australian, Simon Youl, and then Jeremy Bates's service deserted him in the hour of its greatest need against the American doubles specialist, Robert Seguso.

'I don't know what happened,' said Bates after his 6–7, 6–3, 6–2, 6–4 defeat on Court 14, after the solid base he seemed to have developed during a splendidly and competitively played first set disintegrated in the fifth game of the second set. He was crucially and, he must have felt, cruelly broken from 40–15 by three double faults. He double faulted again to go 2–4 down in the third set, and followed it up with yet another double fault calamity on set point. Although he rallied from 0–3 to 3–3 in the fourth set, the damage was done.

Julie Salmon was left as Britain's sole singles survivor out of 22 starters when, after an untidy first set tie-break which ran away from her 7–1, she pulled herself and her game together to beat Adriana Villagran from Argentina 6–7, 6–1, 6–2. Jo Durie should have joined her in the third round. Having been out-hit by South Africa's Ros Fairbank in the first set, she romped through the second and from 0–3 had again raised her game to lead 5–4 in the third. Ten minutes later she was out, beaten 6–2, 1–6, 7–5 by an opponent who was to experience for herself only too well a little later in the tournament how the British player then felt.

Sarah Loosemore's hopes of coming through to play Steffi Graf were ruined by Terry Phelps. The stronger American won 6–1, 6–1 in the sort of routine match which Martina Navratilova, Helena Sukova and Gabriela Sabatini also enjoyed. Not so, however, Chris Evert.

She went uncomfortably close to defeat against Christine Singer, 19, a solidly built West German whose powerful serves and delicate backhands, particularly her drop shots, were very much in the same mould. 'I'm sure defeat crossed my mind, but if it did, then it passed very rapidly,' said Miss Evert. 'For a girl like that to keep serving two aces a game is impossible to keep up. If she played like that normally, we would have heard of her before. She didn't produce the aces on the big points.'

Miss Singer actually had points for 4–3 in the second set but from 2–2 in the third Miss Evert established regal control, with one spell of 12 consecutive points and, from 4–3, another burst of eight to win in the end 6–4, 3–6, 6–3.

Joy for Derrick Rostagno (above) as he beats Marty Davies 16–14 in the fifth, the longest set in this year's tournament.

Happiness too for Czechoslovakia's Petr Korda after knocking out 13th-seeded Emilio Sanchez.

No lack of support for the former champion.

Gently does it by Chris Evert, as she resists an exciting challenge by West Germany's Christina Singer.

A day to remember for Wally Masur and one to forget for John McEnroe.

D A Y

Friday 24 June

The big guns, as represented by Ivan Lendl, Pat Cash, Boris Becker, Henri Leconte and Tim Mayotte, all won on day five but without firing too often on all cylinders. Lendl in particular looked frail but, as he expects a tough match every time he steps on to a grass court, no one should have been unduly surprised when he was extended so fiercely and for so long by Holland's Michiel Schapers.

The fact that Lendl finished so strongly to win 6–7, 7–6, 6–4, 6–7, 6–1 meant that the grim resolution which had been so necessary throughout the three hour 50 minute match on Court 2, where so many other champions or top seeds have allowed the graveyard myth to cloud their judgement, was replaced by a relaxed evaluation of the situation later.

'I was very unhappy that I didn't win in three sets,' he said, citing the 6–5 lead he held in the first set tie-break. 'All I had to do was make a couple of steps to put the ball away, but I slipped, couldn't get to it, dived and he put it away.' Lendl went on to insist that although Schapers, the only player to have taken a set from Cash the year before, levelled the match in the third of their tie-breakers, he was still not worried. 'Unless I beat myself on my own serve, the other guy is always going to have to serve well to beat me,' he continued.

For most of the first four sets Schapers did just that. He also showed a fine touch around the net

Ivan Lendl in full cry against Holland's Michiel Schapers.

Terry Phelps fought determinedly for her four games against Steffi Graf.

Ivan Lendl was stretched to four sets by Michiel Schapers.

Paul Annacone (right) savours victory over an out-of-form and disappointed Jonas Svensson, the 12th seed.

and was quick to pounce when the space was offered for him to hit powerful passing winners. After he critically double-faulted to lose the second game of the final set, though, it was all over. Lendl finished with 18 aces on a court which was cutting up badly. The Dutchman likened it to the rough on a golf course. Lendl, no mean golfer himself, commented, 'In the club I play in at home, the rough doesn't look that bad.'

Becker hit 15 aces as he defeated the American, Sammy Giammalva, on Court 1, but was far from happy with his performance, mainly because he created so many openings and then failed to put the ball away. Giammalva wore a supporting bandage to protect a strained thigh towards the end, and also munched away on bananas during change-overs to give him extra strength. It was the sort of match when such distractions attracted more attention than some of the erratic points.

While Becker was wasting opportunities, Cash was rejoicing in the fact that he was starting to make rather more of his, certainly than in his previous match against Javier Frana, as he beat his good friend and Davis Cup doubles partner, John Fitzgerald, 6–1, 6–2, 6–4.

The man who would be Cash's next challenger suddenly found himself the focus of attention. There may not be any grass courts in the Soviet Union but Andrei Olkhovsky, a qualifier for the second successive year, beat fellow qualifier Chris Pridham from Canada 3–6, 6–3, 6–4, 6–3 for the right to stand between Cash and his projected quarter-final against Becker.

Olkhovsky's success made it the ninth time in 11 years that at least one qualifier had reached the last 16. It was curious to discover that the only match he had won on the Grand Prix circuit before arriving at Wimbledon five days earlier had also been on grass. His strong serve and overheads clearly had much to do with that.

Another qualifier, Barry Moir from South Africa, made Henri Leconte struggle for a while before the Frenchman, who had reached his first Grand Slam final at Roland Garros three weeks earlier, rallied to win 3–6, 6–1, 7–6, 6–1. Although it was easier to reach Court 13 than in some previous years, such is Leconte's appeal that only the faithful, who had arrived early, saw more than brief glimpses of the fun.

Leconte remarked afterwards that he had played three bad sets. 'Everything went wrong. I was terrible, I wasn't moving well and although he doesn't have a big shot, he's always there and he doesn't make mistakes,' said the Frenchman, using those expressive eyes and frowns which paint such evocative pictures of how it must have been on the court, where his mood clearly fluctuated just as much as his tennis.

From the start of the third set tie-break, however, which he strode through 7–0, Leconte was in supreme control. He took the fourth set in a quick-fire 20 minutes to qualify for a fourth round match against Tim Mayotte, whose exemplary serving eventually breached the baseline persistence of Joakim Nystrom, for a 6–4, 4–6, 6–2, 6–4 victory.

The only seed to depart on day five was Jonas Svensson. Looking decidedly weary and short of the variety he likes to bring to his game, the Swede seemed bemused by the renowned tactic of Paul Annacone to seize upon the chance of the chipped return, which then enabled him to move in and angle away the next shot he was offered. Annacone, who reached the quarter-finals as a qualifier in 1984, won 6–4, 6–2, 3–6, 6–4.

Steffi Graf emphatically maintained her part in the two-pronged West German advance in search of both singles trophies as she crushed Terry Phelps, the American who had so ruthlessly swept aside Britain's best junior the day before, 6–3, 6–1.

'I haven't had a tough opponent yet,' observed Miss Graf after winning three matches for the loss of only six games. 'But I'm sure one is going to come along soon.' Miss Phelps, like so many of Miss Graf's opponents during the year and not just in Grand Slam tournaments, seemed intimidated by the very presence of the world champion. The more Miss Graf unleashed that powerful forehand, the easier it became to understand why. Mary Joe Fernandez, the Florida schoolgirl and 16th seed, an easy 6–4, 6–1 winner over Poland's Iwona Kuczynska, would be the next marched in for the top seed's inspection.

Helena Sukova dropped the first set to Japan's Etsuko Inoue but at least she survived, 6–7, 6–3, 6–2. Her former Federation Cup team-mate Hana Mandlikova, now an Australian, after following Martina Navratilova's example in deciding that life as a Czechoslovakian no longer

Henri Leconte ready for an attacking backhand.

Tim Mayotte makes headway against Joakim Nystrom.

suited her, once more fell by the wayside with wasteful haste.

Seven years earlier, when she was a brilliant winner of the French Open and then played equally vibrant tennis to dismiss Miss Navratilova from the semi-finals at Wimbledon, Miss Mandlikova looked set to become a great champion. Instead, so much of her graceful, as well as authoritative, skill has been squandered. She remains the fawn whose nerve is too easily shattered by the slightest disturbance. To be fair, injuries which left her ominously short of match practice contributed to her 6–4, 6–3 defeat by Anne Minter, a born-and-bred Australian, who played as if the question of national supremacy was at stake. 'I don't think of Hana as an Australian yet,' said Miss Minter pointedly.

The match, for all its significance and tense undercurrents, was far from a classic. Mrs Mandlikova, opting to use her married title but her maiden name, served no fewer than five double faults at 3–4 in the second set. There was no escape from that. 'Maybe I don't have the right motivation any more,' she suggested. 'I've been on the circuit for ten years and it's very difficult to come back all the time after injuries. I am not enjoying it as much as I wanted to.'

For a while it looked as if there could be a double celebration for the Minter sisters. Elizabeth took the first set to a tie-break with Zina Garrison, the 1985 semi-finalist, who went on to win 7–6, 6–0.

By now the doubles events, the great lure for those who traditionally flock through the gates of The All England Club at a reduced price after 5 pm, were well under way and the top seeds in both the men's and women's events struggled in uncharacteristic fashion.

Ken Flach and Robert Seguso dropped the first set, albeit only on a tie-break, to Tim Pawsat and Sweden's Tobias Svantesson, who had developed a fine understanding while playing in college tennis together in America, while Martina Navratilova and Pam Shriver were pushed even harder by Jenny Byrne and Janine Thompson.

In fact the Australians held three match points, two at 5–3 and the other when they were serving at 5–4, but Miss Navratilova saved the latter with a blistering return which Miss Byrne volleyed into the net, and the former champions eventually survived 6–4, 3–6, 7–5.

To complete a wonderfully entertaining day's play, Steffi Graf and Gabriela Sabatini had to battle hard and long to rebuff Anne Minter and Holland's Hester Witvoet, who served for the match in the final set but finally went down 7–6, 4–6, 7–5.

One in the eye for Hana Mandlikova, from an ultra-determined Anne Minter.

D A Y

Saturday 25 June

Wimbledon for once had some major competition in the sporting calendar – the final of the
European Soccer Championships in Munich.
Apart from Holland's Menno Oosting, who
hoped his match with Mats Wilander would not
deny him access to a television set when his
countrymen took on the Soviet Union, you
would hardly have noticed. The attendance of
32,449 was an increase on the same day a year
before, and the crowds not only flocked in early
to enjoy the aggressive aperitif which Slobodan
Zivojinovic provided but, after a serving from
Gabriela Sabatini, as sweet as strawberries and
cream in the afternoon, stayed late to gorge
themselves on the day's main attraction, starring
Jimmy Connors.

Oosting missed some of the soccer – but with
Wilander continuing his steadfast progress in a
6–1, 6–4, 6–4 victory he was back in the
dressing room in good time to see Holland
parading round the pitch in Germany with their
trophy. Wilander had far more burgeoning
matters on his mind, such as Zivojinovic, his
opponent for the next round.

'His serve is much better than Becker's,' said
Wilander. 'You can walk about for ten minutes
against Bobo without hitting a shot,' he added,

Weeks of training go into making the perfect
Wimbledon ball boy.

Katrina Adams (right) enjoyed her first Wimbledon, serving and volleying her way to an impressive victory over 15th-seeded Sylvia Hanika.

with the sort of trepidation you might expect from a player with so much at risk against the Yugoslav who beat him in the first round at Wimbledon in 1985 and who had been within two points of denying him the 1988 French Open crown.

For his part, Zivojinovic seemed remarkably laid back about the whole thing. Jelen, who reached the last 16 at Wimbledon in 1986, broke for 3–1 and had two chances to break again in the eighth game, which would have left him serving first in the second set. Yet those few points, which showed Zivojinovic in both his worst and best frames of mind – as three superb winners were scattered between three unforced errors, including two double faults – also proved to be the turning point.

Although Jelen still took the first set, the fact that Zivojinovic had managed to hold two set points against him at 2–5 seemed to remind the Yugoslav of his responsibilities. From then on he was not only starting to make his own serves fly, but he also became far more efficient with his returns. He won 3–6, 6–3, 7–6, 6–3.

The genuine tennis fans were out in force. Stefan Edberg and Ken Flach were given a standing ovation as the Swede, with his increasingly piercing serve and volley game, edged through 6–2, 7–5, 2–6, 7–5 in an exciting three-hour contest on Centre Court. The power within that match was in proper contrast to the glamour earlier, when Miss Sabatini beat the athletic Catherine Tanvier, 6–2, 6–3.

Miss Sabatini was never in danger. Miss Tanvier, who is none the less entertaining and attractive to watch, played many glorious winners in between an equally large number of less subtle shots, which included dozens of forehands which flew yards over the baseline. One of them late into the second set finally roused one of the court coverers who, much to the amusement of the crowd, had slept blissfully through at least five quite lively games.

Several new faces attracted more than a passing glance, among them the happily determined Japanese girl, Akiko Kijimuta, whose clever application of the tactics Chris Evert should have known so well – drop shots followed up by passes – actually strained the legendary American for a while. Miss Kijimuta gave so much in that first set, however, that her energy drained away rapidly in the second, and after charging in forlornly to try and retrieve a

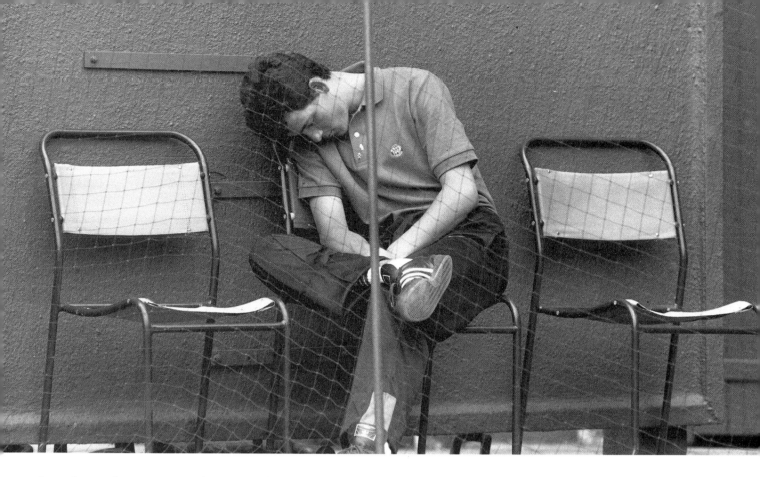

One person at least was oblivious to the excitement on Centre Court, even when Gabriela Sabatini was playing.

teasing drop shot on match point she almost collapsed from exhaustion. The crowd warmly showed its appreciation.

Next for Miss Evert would be Katrina Adams, a serve and volley newcomer, ranked 123 in the world, who had proved too quick and too aggressive at the net for 15th-seeded Sylvia Hanika from West Germany, winning 6–3, 6–3. Meanwhile 10th-seeded Lori McNeil, no longer playing with the zest and freshness of spirit which helped her beat Miss Evert at the US Open the previous September, went down 7–6, 6–4 to Ros Fairbank.

Those upsets apart, the women's singles was following its mainly expected pattern, with nine of the last 16 moving into the second week without losing a set. They included two Russians, Natalia Zvereva and Larisa Savchenko. The latter, with her first-class backhand and general supremacy all round the court, ended much honest and earnest battling by Britain's lone survivor at this stage, Julie Salmon. Court 14 was packed to overflowing with patriotic supporters, but for the 194th player in the world rankings, against the 19th, that was never likely to be enough.

Miss Salmon did not help matters with nine double faults, but at least she had the consolation of winning £4,500 – more than she had earned in the rest of the year. She also retained her sense of humour. 'It's back to the park in Brighton for daily practice in front of a group of old grannies,' she said.

Back with the men's singles, Wally Masur followed up his defeat of John McEnroe with another lively, spirited performance and a 6–4, 6–4, 6–7, 6–1 victory over Robert Seguso. No hidden fears for him on Court 2.

His success meant that there would be six unseeded players in the last 16, three of them Australians. Mark Woodforde, who had underlined his pedigree with victories over Johan Kriek, Ramesh Krishnan and the volatile Diego Nargiso, was already there, while Simon Youl joined them when his extra grass court experience told against the slim Czechoslovakian left-hander, Petr Korda.

Also through unseeded was the West German, Patrick Kuhnen, another whose obvious ability to play on grass had remained hidden in the past. After his surprisingly comprehensive 6–1, 6–4, 6–4 defeat of Jim Grabb, Kuhnen said – somewhat tongue in cheek, it seemed at the

Pam Shriver survives two tie-break sets to beat Stephanie Rehe.

Mats Wilander made quick work of Menno Oosting.

Stefan Edberg (right) maintained the pressure against Ken Flach.

time – that he hoped Jimmy Connors would beat Derrick Rostagno to provide him with his next opponent, because 'beating Connors will earn me more bonus points on the ranking list than beating Rostagno'. His wish, we now know, was granted – but only just.

Jimmy Connors, that most practised exponent of the tightrope, especially at Wimbledon in recent years, kept Court 1 in the most gripping suspense before he eventually emerged victorious 7–5, 4–6, 4–6, 6–2, 7–5 after four hours and two minutes.

A year earlier, on Centre Court, Connors produced the performance of The Championships, if not of the whole 1987 circuit, with his recovery from two sets and 1–4 down against Mikael Pernfors. 'Then they were throwing sand on my grave,' the old warrior joked later. 'This time I wasn't down so far.' When he was two sets to one down and had to save five break points on his serve in the fourth set, it certainly started to look as if it was time to man the lifeboat.

It arrived, needless to say, in the shape of Connors's own uncanny survival instinct, carried along by those wondrous passing shots hit in full flight, which have so long been the hallmark of a career which could surely one day be the basis for a Superman tennis fantasy.

The fourth set was absolutely critical. Connors saved three break points in the opening game and two more in the fifth, to defy an opponent who was not only serving wide and well but winning many points with great touch around the net. Yet Rostagno was stunned and then broken by two Connors shots down the line, one a forehand, the other a backhand, as the former champion held on. The Californian then double-faulted three times in his next service game to set the scene for a rousing finale.

Serving for the match Connors saved three break points, the first with another of many fantastic lobs. The atmosphere was almost unbearable. A smash took Connors to match point but Rostagno, who had clawed his way back from 5–2, saved it with a net cord which led to the ball literally dribbling into the American's territory.

When Connors then double-faulted and Rostagno made it 5–5 it began to look as if there would be no dream ending after all, for either the crowd, Connors or the waiting Kuhnen. It was 7.15 pm. The sun, which had been hidden for so long, suddenly reappeared and Connors reached match point for a second time, with one of those backhand returns which have experience and class written all over them.

Rostagno, who was born in Hollywood and played far more than just a supporting role in this epic, then double-faulted. It was a tragic ending, but Rostagno's epigraph on the way Connors had brought a stimulating, rather than constantly spectacular, first week to a close was worth preserving.

'If you don't appreciate Connors, you don't appreciate the game of tennis. He comes up with things that nobody's ever done before and does them so solidly, so casually. Good tennis is an art and he's an artist. One of the joys of tennis is that it can change at any time. He has a great return, one of the best I've ever played against, and when he's down he just comes back and plays better. It's incredible. In the fourth set I thought I played a great set, but for 15 consecutive points he played unbelievable tennis. It was great to see him and it was great to be on the other side, even though I lost the set 6–2.'

Clear delight all round as Stephen Shaw (left) and John Lloyd upset Paul Annacone and Christo Van Rensburg, the seventh seeds.

A classic two-fisted shot from former champion Jimmy Connors, which had Derrick Rostagno at full stretch.

D A Y
7

Monday 27 June

The seventh day's cast list could hardly have been richer. With a full line-up of fourth round men's and women's singles topping the bill, seven of the top eight seeds in both events still involved and 10 countries still represented, everything was poised for the most thrilling second week at Wimbledon for years.

An 'abundance of talent' as referee Alan Mills called it, was spread all around the show courts, with Gabriela Sabatini, Pam Shriver, Natalia Zvereva, Stefan Edberg, Jimmy Connors and, most excitingly of all for the crowds lacking tickets for Centre Court or Court 1, defending champion Pat Cash among those playing outside.

Cash, who had already played twice on Centre Court and once on Court 1, raised no objection to playing on Court 14. He accepted that even Wimbledon champions have to be reminded of what it is like in the 'country'. At the same time he was greatly relieved when he served an ace on his third match point to end a memorable Wimbledon for Andrei Olkhovsky, so that he could return, after his customary distribution of headbands, to the relative sanctuary of the dressing room.

The Pat Cash fan club hail their hero on Court 14.

'It was like a zoo out there,' said Cash after his 6–3, 6–3, 6–3 victory. 'It's a good thing that the kids can come and watch me, but I wish someone would tell them how distracting it can be to use a flash camera when I'm serving. In circumstances like that, there is always the possibility of an upset.'

As it happened, although there were two surprises in the women's singles, neither made as much impact as the one which almost happened on Court 1, where Ivan Lendl had to save a match point before overcoming the unseeded Australian, Mark Woodforde, 7–5, 6–7, 6–7, 7–5, 10–8 after four hours 46 minutes – the longest match, by one minute, of the 1988 Championships.

The ginger-haired, freckle-faced left-hander whom Australians naturally hope may one day become as successful as a certain Rod Laver who possessed those same qualities and many more, fought with immense courage, skill and dignity to try and bridge the gap between being 54th and first in the world rankings.

At 7–6 in the final set there was a real chance that he might do so. He had so coolly saved one break point in the sixth game and two more in the tenth, either with tremendous serves or by defiantly moving into the net and literally tempting Lendl to go for a risky pass. Now he was one point from the greatest moment of his career.

'C'mon,' the crowd heard Woodforde urge himself, after he had struck yet another of his stunning backhand service returns to put the world champion on the rack. Yet Lendl, who eight times in the previous seven years had come through to win in five sets, though never before from match point down, responded with the strength of character one would expect. The serve was strong and accurate; the volley which followed landed perfectly and unreturnably in Woodforde's backhand corner.

In the end it was Lendl's extraordinary fitness and stamina, which he has worked so selflessly to achieve, which saved him in his second successive five-setter. 'It was survival of the toughest and unfortunately I wasn't the toughest,' said Woodforde who, apart from the match point, also had two points for the first set, both after Lendl had double-faulted. In all Lendl served 25 aces and 21 double faults, including the 17th when he first served at 5–4 for the fourth set. Woodforde made it 5–5 but a severe

Mark Woodforde was one tantalizing point away from beating the top seed, Ivan Lendl.

Quick-change artist Barbara Potter had problems with the heat before her departure (above right) in the last 16.

lapse of concentration in the game which followed was a salutary lesson.

He had been frustrated by a player who, as he said, 'always came up with something at those extreme moments. He just kept serving bombs and I had great difficulty in returning them. The first serves were nuclear rockets, the second serves just rockets.'

Meanwhile, before rain and bad light left Jimmy Connors and Patrick Kuhnen in suspense overnight at a set all and 6–6, Tim Mayotte comfortably in control with a two sets lead over Henri Leconte, and Boris Becker and Paul Annacone prevented from even reaching Court 1, the Swedish machine rolled on. Mats Wilander had clearly prepared and plotted well to make sure there would be no firework serving display by Slobodan Zivojinovic this time. He allowed the burly Yugoslav only seven points on his own serve in the first set, and although the second then went to a tie-break, Wilander was quick to remind everyone who was in charge, by taking it 7–1. Towards the end of Wilander's 6–4, 7–6, 7–5 victory, as he began to put away volleys of real quality, it was hard to believe that he, rather than Zivojinovic, was the one who was unsure about playing on grass.

Stefan Edberg competently stayed on course in straight sets at the expense of Simon Youl, while Miloslav Mecir, though still wearing a corset to protect his back, continued his almost unnoticed progress through to the quarter-finals and a fascinating tilt at Wilander, by beating Wally Masur 4–6, 6–2, 6–4, 6–2.

On clay, Gabriela Sabatini can be lethal, as she had twice proved earlier in the year by scoring the only victories registered over Steffi Graf. On grass, it can be an entirely different matter as Zina Garrison demonstrated when the 12th seed beat the fifth, 6–1, 3–6, 6–2. It could have been even more clear-cut. Miss Garrison, who until this tournament had not enjoyed the best of times in 1988, led 5–0 in the final set and spurned four match points before celebrating her triumph, which avenged an extraordinary 6–0, 6–0 defeat for her at their last meeting.

That had been at Hilton Head, South Carolina, in April and now Miss Garrison commented, 'I'd thought about nothing else for three days and nights. Winning the first game was the biggest relief you can imagine. It was like having an explosion inside. It felt that good.'

Miss Garrison's tennis is a bit like that. She

has spells when her exciting serve and volley game looks irresistible and then times when the whole fabric of her tennis falls apart. As for Miss Sabatini, she could do little more than cry for Argentina. She admitted that after five months away from her homeland she longed to return for a rest.

The other seeding upset was the straight sets defeat of Natalia Zvereva, the Russian runner-up at the French Open, by Ros Fairbank, although, as with the Garrison success, it was one which was always on the cards on this surface. Miss Fairbank won 6–2, 6–4 and, like Miss Garrison, endured something of a nervous flutter when Miss Zvereva, hitting out freely at last, recovered from 0–4 to 4–4 in the second set.

'All week I've been saying it would be great if I could get through and play Martina Navratilova. I've never really come close to beating her, but I'm playing well and look forward to playing her. It will be fun,' Miss Fairbank said. In the event it was not exactly 'fun' for either of them, but for the moment Miss Navratilova had other things on her mind. With rain blurring the vision through her spectacles, she slipped to 4–2 against Larisa Savchenko before her match was also delayed overnight.

Meanwhile Pam Shriver had dealt conclusively enough with Katerina Maleeva; Helena Sukova, in two solidly played sets, ensured that there was no need for a posse of photographers to remain any longer on permanent sentry duty waiting for Barbara Potter to change her shirt; and Pascale Paradis ousted Anne Minter to become a Grand Slam quarter-finalist for the first time.

For her part, Steffi Graf provided The Princess of Wales with a reminder of the stunning forehand power she had experienced at first hand three weeks earlier when they played doubles against each other at the opening of the new European offices of the Women's International Tennis Association.

That forehand played its typically convincing part as Miss Graf overwhelmed the American teenager Mary Joe Fernandez, seeded 16, who said plaintively, 'It's tough to play her, she's so fast. Before you know it, the ball is coming back at you. Most of the points were bang, bang.'

Chris Evert had another physically daunting struggle before beating Katrina Adams, 19, from Chicago, 5–7, 6–3, 6–0. The sturdily built Miss Adams (coached like Zina Garrison by John Wilkerson) went for Miss Evert's attacking shots with a fine flourish as she produced what she called the best set she had ever played, to have American journalists scurrying towards Court 2.

In particular she hit some especially fine low volleys, which belied a world ranking of 125, before Miss Evert's lobbing, which had been damagingly short in the first set, eventually found the depth it needed and she started mixing up the play in the way she knows best.

Like the delightful Japanese girl, Akiko Kijimuta, in the previous round, Miss Adams put so much into the first set that 'mentally and physically I ran out of gas. I just got worn down.' They join a large company of Miss Evert's challengers who, over 17 years, have said the same.

Above: Zina Garrison's more fluent strokes on grass were too much for an increasingly bemused Gabriela Sabatini (above left).

A gritty determination helped Ros Fairbank (bottom right) beat 17-year-old top Russian prospect Natalia Zvereva.

Pensive thoughts in the Royal Box, as R.E.H. 'Buzzer' Hadingham (left), Chairman of The All England Club, The Princess of Wales and (second from right) The Duchess of York watch Mats Wilander (right) beat Slobodan Zivojinovic.

Mary Joe Fernandez could not cope with Steffi Graf's power.

Once again Miloslav Mecir has placed his shot to perfection as he ends Wally Masur's fine run.

D A Y 8

Tuesday 28 June

Just as a few days earlier the truth was hard to bear for John McEnroe, so it was for Jimmy Connors when, almost inevitably, the years caught up with him. For once the energy, the spark and the inspiration were missing, even after an overnight rest, as he went out, far from quietly, against Patrick Kuhnen, the baker's son from West Germany.

Disappointingly, too, on one of those days when the tongue was mightier than the racket, there was a good deal of self-denigration embroidered by obscenities which, even if they had been addressed about the weather which held up the proceedings until the early evening, did nothing to help the former champion's game or reputation.

As a parting shot after his 5–7, 7–6, 7–6, 6–7, 6–3 defeat by an opponent who was simply fitter and faster than he was, Connors said of Court 2, which has become known as 'the graveyard of the champions': 'It's a pain in the ass court and a pain in the ass to play out there.'

The harsh reality was that having given 100 per cent and even more in fighting spirit and energy to fend off Derrick Rostagno in his previous match, Connors could not lift himself to another super-human, super-charged display so soon again afterwards. At 35 the powers of recovery take that much longer.

In an astonishing collapse of spirit and will, Connors lost the last 12 points of the match from 3–3 in the fifth set as the tall, curly-haired Kuhnen followed up those mighty serves, which had done so much damage throughout the contest, with short-angled volleys of real quality and some surprisingly lethal backhands.

Two points before the American seemed almost prepared to accept defeat, he had half a chance, at 3–2 and 30–30. But it vanished, and once Kuhnen had broken him in the seventh game with another of his stinging returns, there was nothing left but for Connors to complain, not just about his own state but also about that of the court.

Basically his chance vanished within minutes of the resumption of play after reaching a set all and 6–6 the night before. Most would have expected the more experienced Connors to win the instant tie-break. Instead it was Kuhnen, hitting groundstrokes cleanly and penetratingly, who immediately found his range, touch and timing to take the game 7–2. Those extra bonus ranking points were to be his.

Because of the weather, this was essentially a tidying-up day in the men's singles, while completing the line-up for the quarter-finals. That Mats Wilander would play Miloslav Mecir we already knew; Kuhnen's next giant-killing would be directed at Stefan Edberg. That still left Boris Becker to take his place against Pat Cash and Tim Mayotte against top-seeded Ivan Lendl.

Becker, who over the weekend had received a personal letter from The All England Club Chairman, R. E. H. 'Buzzer' Hadingham, more or less urging him to ignore the uncomplimentary adjectives used by some of the British tabloid newspapers to describe him, hardly seemed bothered by anything as he swept aside the unseeded Paul Annacone 6–3, 6–4, 6–4.

In fact he described this as the perfect build-up for the forthcoming heavyweight showdown with Cash. Becker's power play, especially on serve, was evident in his defeat of Annacone in one hour 53 minutes, although the simple thought that this was a quick match underlined only too graphically how long even they take these days. It still took nearly four minutes per game. Becker, with his vastly improved returns, made one service break in each set. That was sufficient. For the first time since 1964, when it was Christian Kuhnke and Wilhelm Bungert, two West Germans had made it to the last eight.

80

The saddest scene of all.

Connors was not the only player who surrendered with surprising tameness on this second Tuesday. So too did Henri Leconte who, despite making an initially brave attempt to retrieve an overnight deficit of two sets to tenth-seeded Mayotte, then crumpled under the extra weight, accuracy and control of the American's volleying.

Mayotte, who surged to 4–0 in the fourth set to deny Leconte any chance of continuing his comeback, went on to reach the quarter-finals for a fifth time with a 6–4, 7–6, 4–6, 6–2 victory.

While waiting for the weather to clear, the crowd enjoyed some unscheduled diversions, including the sudden appearance of a juggler in the Centre Court open stand and then an interview with Fred Perry, which was broadcast over the public address system and included a straw poll that gave overwhelming support for grass courts to remain the pride and joy at Wimbledon.

When play did eventually resume, Martina Navratilova quickly banished her frustration and irritation of the night before to take her belated place in the quarter-finals, while Chris Evert, Steffi Graf and Pam Shriver all advanced, as the seedings said they would, into the semi-finals.

The defending champion took only 39 minutes to transform her troubling 2–4 overnight deficit against the sturdy, often hard-hitting Russian, Larisa Savchenko, into a 6–4, 6–2 victory. While waiting to go on court, she had watched a Vietnam war film and a recording of Mike Tyson's 91-second demolition of Michael Spinks in Atlantic City in the early hours of that morning. 'Tyson never took a step back and that was so inspiring,' said Miss Navratilova of the heavyweight champion.

The same could be said about her. Dancing about the court with obvious eagerness she took five successive games, to banish any idea that Miss Savchenko (like her doubles partner, Natalia Zvereva, in Paris) might cause another sensational upset. With that defeat still rankling, Miss Navratilova grinned and said, 'I'm on a mission against all Russians now. That's my idea of *glasnost*.'

Pam Shriver claimed she had eaten breakfast three times before she eventually started what became a 6–4, 6–4 defeat of Zina Garrison. It seemed to have done her good, and clearly whatever Chris Evert took for sustenance during the long delay also had the right effect when she played Helena Sukova.

Miss Evert can be a notoriously slow starter; Miss Sukova the reverse. On this occasion all such predictions went out of the window. It was Miss Evert who, with the minimum of fuss or ceremony, started serving with authority and punishing the Czechoslovakian severely for too many far from subtle approaches to the net. Miss Evert won the first set in 30 minutes, and although Miss Sukova's resistance strengthened, helped by several aces, it was another crucial error on a backhand approach in the tie-break which enabled the American to sew things up 6–3, 7–6.

That left just Miss Graf who, after being alerted to play three times, only to find that the weather had deteriorated again, was in the middle of a game of cards when eventually she was called to take on the French former world junior champion, Pascale Paradis. 'After sitting around all day it took me longer than usual to get into the match,' said Miss Graf, even though she needed only 49 minutes to complete a 6–3, 6–1 victory.

She then admitted that she was becoming slightly concerned lest the speed and ease with which she was racing through her matches, none of them over an hour, might tell against her in the tougher tests she still expected to come. 'My opponents haven't been as strong as their ranking would indicate,' she remarked. 'I've not yet been threatened. I'm having to practise a lot more between matches, on top of my usual routine.'

Helena Sukova once again found Chris Evert just too clever and tenacious for her.

Tim Mayotte quickly established his supremacy over Henri Leconte (right), who did not have the best of luck.

There was no lack of impromptu entertainment for the crowds when rain held up play. This character proved himself a juggler, as well as a clown.

'Just what I needed,' Martina Navratilova tells herself after recovering overnight from 2–4 to beat Larisa Savchenko.

A hair-raising experience for Zina Garrison (above right), as she loses to Pam Shriver in the quarter-finals.

Pascale Paradis found the strength she needed against Anne Minter, to reach her first Grand Slam tournament quarter-final.

When play at last was possible Jimmy Connors, for once, was kept on the run by West German newcomer Patrick Kuhnen.

DAY 9

Wednesday 29 June

One champion fell by the wayside, the other escaped just as the guillotine seemed sure to fall. This was a remarkable day, when any Grand Slam hopes which may have been starting to germinate in Mats Wilander's mind also became enmeshed in the maddeningly deceptive web which Miloslav Mecir can weave, when he is in the mood.

For many, the quarter-final clash between defending champion Pat Cash and his immediate predecessor, Boris Becker, was as good as the final. The winner of this battle, the spectators decided in goodly numbers, would almost certainly go on to claim this year's title.

Becker, who was wise enough to keep reminding everyone prepared to listen that it takes seven matches to win Wimbledon, not five, certainly played as if it was the most crucial and difficult hurdle he had to overcome, in 'the most important tournament in the world'. After striking the last of countless crunching service winners to complete a spectacularly aggressive 6–4, 6–3, 6–4 triumph, Becker leapt high in the air with understandable elation.

'If you play the defending champion, you obviously have to play at your best to beat him. That's what I did today,' said the West German. Having banished the memory of Peter Doohan and what happened to him last year, Becker was immediately made the odds-on favourite by the bookmakers to take the Wimbledon crown

for a third time in four years.

Just as Becker predicted, the match was played and won as much in the head as in the hands and feet, although it was significant too that Cash could not serve as well as he needed to, and therefore had fewer opportunities to demonstrate those quick-fire reflexes at the net which were so beneficial for him in 1987.

One had to remember, too, that despite his optimistic observations after earlier matches, Cash had not won a tournament since the previous November. The first set was vital for them both and in the tenth game, three volleying errors – the last and most unsettling of them on set point – began to sow those destructive seeds of doubt within the Australian, despite the fact that he had started the set with his fifth ace.

'After that first set I could feel that on the big points he was nervous, and that gave me the inspiration to break him again right at the start of the second,' said Becker. 'That was the difference.' Becker's mental mastery was emphasized still further when Cash had so many chances in the third set. He let slip two break points in the second game, broke later for 4–2 on a Becker double fault but then, despite two stunning backhand passes, double-faulted twice to allow the West German to bounce straight back one game later.

There were moments when these two young lions of the modern game were not exactly on the same wavelength. After an exchange of drop shots in the sixth game of the fourth set, Cash cut off a Becker forehand and the momentum carried him, head first, over the net. Becker walked up and did the same. 'Something came over me and I did it too. It was just fun,' he said. Cash clearly did not think so. By the end of the fortnight others were left wondering about the ethics of the incident as well.

Cash kept his so-called joke for later. He presented himself in the interview room wearing a wild, reddish, punk-style wig, saying, 'If you can't beat 'em, join 'em.' It transpired later that his original idea was to beat the West German and then present the wig as Becker's scalp.

For the seventh time in their 11 meetings Wilander, the reigning Australian and French Open champion, was left completely baffled and beaten by Mecir, the Czechoslovakian who, on his good days – and this was certainly one of them – justifies such nicknames as 'The Big Cat' and 'The Conjurer'.

With that loping stride and enormous reach carrying him with surprising speed about the court with what often seems like a minimum of effort, and delivering beguiling shots to parts of the court which others cannot reach, Mecir produced two hours of classically skilful tennis for his 6–3, 6–1, 6–3 victory on the Centre Court.

A shy but immensely likeable man, who prefers to let his racket do most of the talking, Mecir had Wilander mentally and physically trapped from the moment he saved three key break points in an opening game which lasted ten minutes. Two games later the torture which Wilander feared began.

He started making more and more errors in trying to deal with balls which were keeping low, and confusion set in. He tried to vary his tactics but Mecir was always waiting, always one step and reach ahead. It was marvellous to watch; misery to endure for Wilander, who had played so brilliantly to take the sting out of Zivojinovic's threat the round before.

Yet the other surviving Swede, Stefan Edberg, as inscrutable and unemotional as ever, marched on with just one lapse of concentration in his 6–3, 4–6, 6–1, 7–6 defeat of the Connors conqueror, Patrick Kuhnen. Kuhnen was certainly persistent and, despite a double fault to concede the first set, his powerful serving remained a nagging problem for Edberg. Deservedly he levelled the match when sharp returns forced the third seed to err at the net, and it needed a series of fine passing shots from Edberg to reassert his control.

Lendl, admitting he was lucky still to be involved after his narrow escape against Mark Woodforde, duly beat Tim Mayotte, as he always had done in the past. The score was 7–6, 7–6, 6–3, making it 12–0 for Lendl in matches and, just as importantly, 10–0 in tie-breaks.

Those statistics, rather than the memory of

Anything you can do, I can do better, insists Boris Becker, before picking himself up to beat the defending champion.

A coolly assured backhand by Boris Becker against an obviously apprehensive Pat Cash, as the Australian could sense the title slipping away from him.

how he pressed Lendl to 9–7 in the fifth set the last time they played at Wimbledon in 1986, were probably biting into Mayotte's mind each time they reached a sudden-death situation in the first two sets on this occasion.

Mayotte won only two points in the first set tie-break and one of those was disputed by Lendl, who claimed that a backhand return down the line had dropped out. The second tie-break was taken even more decisively, 7–1, by the Czechoslovakian, who had hoped to be an American citizen by now.

Yet with hindsight the most vital incident and, from Lendl's point of view, the most exasperating, came when he had to take an injury time-out at 6–5 in the first set for treatment to a thigh injury. At the time it did not appear to be serious. In the event it was to be the beginning of the end of his tenth bid to add the men's singles title to the junior boys' title that he won at Wimbledon in 1978.

So the semi-final line-up came down to Lendl v Becker and Edberg v Mecir, and Rex Bellamy of *The Times* could not resist pointing out that 'There will be no Cash but (for the first time) two Czechs' involved.

Just one remaining women's singles quarter-final needed to be wrapped up, and what a match it was before Martina Navratilova, riding out an inordinate amount of luck, squeezed herself free of one looming disaster after another to beat Ros Fairbank, 4–6, 6–4, 7–5. Miss Fairbank, ranked 50th in the world, set Court 14 alight by taking the first set from 0–3 down and holding points for 5–2 in both the second and third sets. Not only was the 24-seat Press Box full, with others waiting from the very first point, but the video room, providing closed-circuit coverage, was packed to capacity.

When serving at 4–2 and 40–30 in the second set, Miss Fairbank, 27, from Durban but living in San Diego, completely missed what was supposed to be a forehand volley. 'I had my chances and missed them,' she lamented later.

'That was her only choke shot in the whole match,' said Miss Navratilova. 'She froze on it and pushed it wide. When she had those points for 5–2, I thought I would lose. But I refused to lose, I never stopped believing that I would somehow pull through and perhaps go on to win the tournament. That kept me going but I was still thinking, "What a way to go. Not now, please – not on Court 14."'

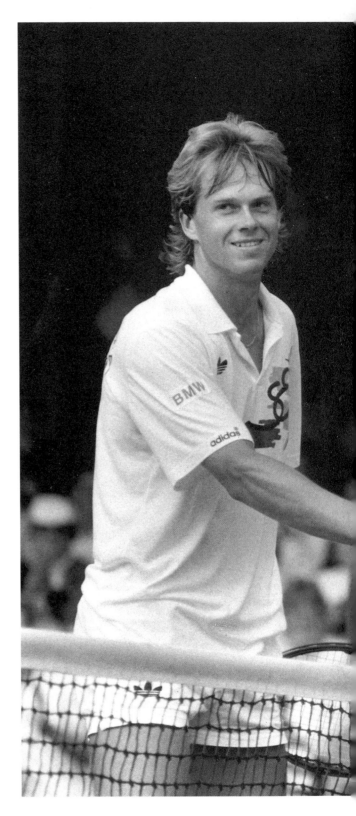

The faces tell it all, as Stefan Edberg marches on against Patrick Kuhnen.

Ros Fairbank (above) held points to lead 5–2 in both the second and third sets against Martina Navratilova . . . but the defending champion's resolute fighting spirit pulled her through in the end.

Having escaped in the singles, however, Miss Navratilova and Pam Shriver, the top seeds, were beaten later in the women's doubles, which they had won together on five previous occasions. They went out, for the second successive year, to opponents from the Soviet Union. In 1987 they had lost to Svetlana Parkhomenko and Larisa Savchenko. This time Miss Savchenko played with Natalia Zvereva, a new combination being prepared for the Olympic Games, and they beat the Americans 7–6, 6–2.

Meanwhile in the men's doubles the holders, Ken Flach and Robert Seguso, also had a

Life can be tough. Mark Woodforde lost a match point against the top seeds in singles and doubles.

tremendous struggle but produced some outstanding tennis as they recovered from two sets and match point down against the Australians Wally Masur and Mark Woodforde. It was a bitter irony for Woodforde. He had been within a point of beating not only the top-seeded singles player (Lendl) but the top-seeded team in the doubles as well.

One at a time, please! Natalia Zvereva (right) ready to back up her doubles partner, Larisa Savchenko.

Pat Cash, seen here with Anne-Britt and son Daniel, had hoped to claim the scalp of Boris Becker. Instead it was a case of 'If you can't beat 'em, join 'em' for a despondent falling champion, as Becker celebrated.

Mats Wilander (left) had to endure another painful
lesson from Miloslav Mecir.

Tim Mayotte had fully justified his tenth seeding but
then found Ivan Lendl an altogether tougher opponent
to break down.

DAY 10

Thursday 30 June

The women's semi-finals in 1988 brought together the same pairings as in 1987. The course of the matches and their outcome were much the same as well – at least almost. A year earlier Chris Evert had fought back with typical resilience to take the second set, and eventually lost without any of the heartbreak surrounding the final point this time.

In fact, although the line-call which caused all the fuss was probably a correct one, the climax to this 78th contest between two great champions, who have so often added to the record books in women's tennis, was accompanied by boos, jeers and slow hand-clapping.

Miss Evert, having already saved three match points in a match which had grown from one of the patchiest to one of the most compelling they had played, was convinced she had prised back a fourth with the crosscourt forehand she had played. It clipped the net, eluded her opponent and dropped quickly by the sideline. Miss Evert gave a little skip of delight in thinking she had kept the match alive.

In fact, with Miss Navratilova swinging round to look and saying to herself, 'Call it out, linesman . . . please . . .' the official, though a trifle late, did just that. After further hesitation, which was really the nub of the problem, the umpire told the still-disbelieving Miss Evert, 'The ball was out.'

For about 20 seconds as the players just looked at each other from opposite ends of the court, the crowd demonstrated its annoyance. How much of it was, though, as Miss Evert said later 'a mixture of hoping and seeing' on her part, as well as on the part of the crowd, one will never know.

Miss Navratilova commented, 'It was a shame, after it had been so close, for it to end that way. I should have won it on the point before but I tripped over my feet. Chris thought the ball was good. When the ball came through, I thought it would be in, but when it clipped the net, I thought it would be out. I can't say it was good. I can't say it was out. What was I supposed to do?'

Certainly all the sympathy lay with Miss Evert, 33, who again played with great skill and defiance, after a first set which left her heading for what might easily have been her worst Wimbledon defeat. She was undoubtedly the favourite with the crowd, as these two leading ladies of the tennis theatre fought with increasing intensity to steal the spotlight and earn the loudest cheers on the stage they know and love best.

The feeling was not lost on Miss Navratilova, now only one match away from that record ninth title which clearly meant so much to her. When she was asked if the uncertainty and controversy over the final point had stopped the crowd from applauding her victory, she raised her eyebrows and said, 'Applaud me? Surely you jest. I thought I was a Martian out there, but I don't care. I don't play this tournament for them.'

Both players claimed it was one of the best matches they had played. It was hardly that. The first set was littered with errors, as if both were having difficulty in remembering those lines at which they were once instinctively word perfect. One unkind soul even suggested it was more like a semi-retirement than a semi-final.

Yet the longer it lasted, especially after a 70-minute break for rain, the richer it became, with the third set a real delight except for the last point, of course. Miss Navratilova broke for 3–1 but Miss Evert promptly broke back, and at 4–5 came the finest game of this, and probably any other, match during the women's tournament.

Chris Evert playing Martina Navratilova for the 78th time.

An overhit backhand off a drop shot gave Miss Navratilova match point, but when she chipped and charged her on the next point there was Miss Evert waiting with a perfectly driven forehand pass worthy of a Grade A in any tennis history examination.

Miss Evert eventually held, but at 5–6 she found herself facing three more match points. She saved the first with a backhand as familiar as her signature, the second with a lob. Then came that call from the sideline that it was all over.

Will the three times champion return for yet another Wimbledon? 'I don't know,' she said. 'Although I'm disappointed now, I'll have forgotten about it in a couple of days.'

Looking ahead to the final, Miss Evert tipped Steffi Graf because, as both she and Ros Fairbank had shown, the defending champion was still not looking entirely comfortable. Miss Shriver, despite taking one more game from the West German and keeping her on court for eight more minutes than in 1987, said she felt 'intimidated' by Miss Graf's power and pace while losing 6–1, 6–2.

That was not a bad assessment. She had just experienced the improvements which Miss Graf had constructed around her serve, her backhand and even that awesome forehand in the previous 12 months. She broke Miss Shriver's opening service game with the assistance of a double fault on her third break point, and sailed on to the final having conceded only 17 games in six matches. Miss Navratilova, who yielded only 26 games while winning The Championships in 1983, had by comparison lost 43 games. She had extended her run of winning matches to 47, but it was the next one that really mattered.

The weather had played havoc with the doubles and the ancillary events, but at least the men's doubles was progressing well and the defending champions kept a sizeable Centre Court crowd enthralled until 8.39 pm by a remarkable third set tie-break, which took them once more into the final.

Flach and Seguso eventually beat Eddie Edwards and Gary Muller, unseeded South Africans who had already won four tie-breaks in earlier rounds, 6–4, 6–4, 7–6, (14–12). Edwards and Muller saved six match points during the tie-break but also squandered a set point of their own, before Flach intercepted a service return with a punching backhand volley to complete the match.

Flach thought he had won it moments earlier when he hit a blistering service backhand return down the line. He raced triumphantly to the net only to be told that the ball had drifted out. It did not matter quite as much as the shot from Chris Evert which had dropped over another Centre Court line a few hours earlier.

Chris Evert fought to the last . . .

. . . but then came the controversy over the final point, with an anxious moment for Martina Navratilova before the call which confirmed her victory.

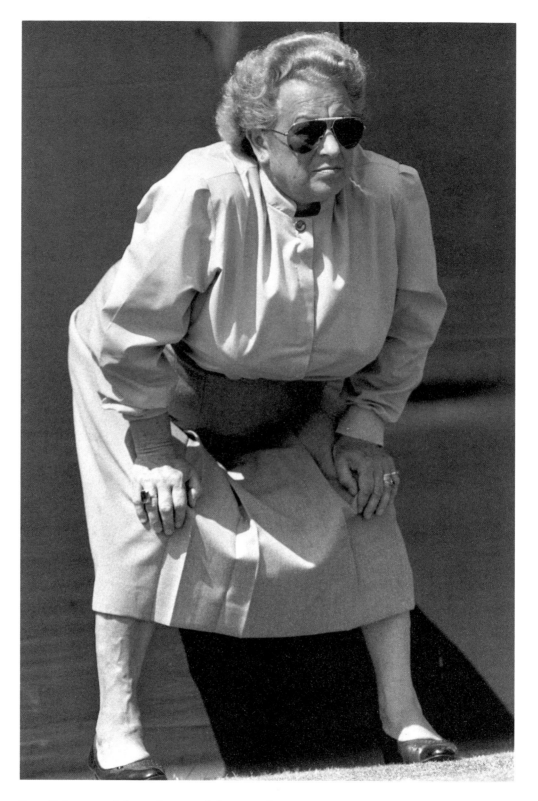

Geta Cole, one of the stalwarts of the British Tennis Umpires Association.

Head groundsman Jim Thorn tidies up.

Pam Shriver seems to have that 'I've been in this situation before' look as, for the second successive year, she loses to Steffi Graf in the semi-finals.

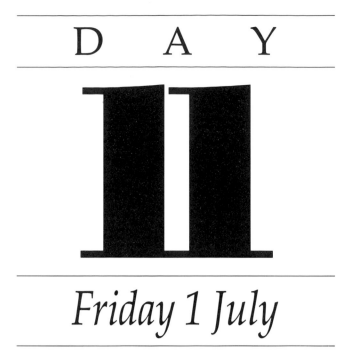

D A Y
11

Friday 1 July

By the time gathering gloom ended play on the eleventh day of these Championships we still did not know who would be competing in the men's singles final. Stefan Edberg was already there, almost incredibly as it happened, because at one stage in the afternoon he had been trailing by two sets and several break points to Miloslav Mecir.

His opponent for the title, however, would not be decided until Boris Becker, the favourite, and Ivan Lendl, increasingly handicapped by a pulled thigh muscle, continued their unfinished business on the following day. At 9.02 pm, after Lendl had courageously saved three match points in a third set tie-break to keep his chances of taking the title tantalizingly alive, their contest was adjourned with the West German leading by two sets to one.

They had already spent two hours and 46 minutes producing often violent tennis before Lendl managed to stay alive in a 10–8 tie-break, which was very nearly as dramatic as the 18–16 epic between John McEnroe and Bjorn Borg in 1980. McEnroe won that set but lost the match. Lendl, we were to discover later, suffered the same disappointment.

Before all that excitement happened, and 75 minutes after he seemed to be stumbling to semi-final defeat for the second successive year, Edberg was celebrating the most remarkable tournament comeback of his already impressive

Becker after he had trimmed that fringe.

114

Boris Becker and Ivan Lendl did not even have time to start their delayed men's singles semi-final before rain drove them off again.

For two sets Miloslav Mecir was completely in charge against Stefan Edberg.

Stefan Edberg can hardly believe he has won, as he slowly sinks down the back canvas while savouring the joy of reaching his first Wimbledon final.

career. For a player who was supposed to lack courage, he picked himself up off the floor several times, dusted himself down and then applied a resounding fifth set knock-out to beat the Czechoslovakian 4–6, 2–6, 6–4, 6–3, 6–4.

In the first nine games of that critical third set Mecir possessed six break points, three in the third game and three more in the seventh. When the service line monitor went off unintentionally after the first point of that game, Edberg shook his head dismally, as if he sensed disaster. Instead it signalled the start of his magnificent recovery.

Suddenly, in the tenth game of that set, as Edberg broke to love with a stream of sparkling service returns, 'The Big Cat' drew his claws in. For two and a half hours he had largely been in control. Edberg, who double-faulted to 0–30 and encouraged Mecir to follow up with beautiful passing winners to break for 5–4 in the first set, looked increasingly dispirited.

He could not read the majority of Mecir's returns quickly enough to make sure that the next gap which his opponent decided to attack

would be covered. Mecir was playing the perfect tune, with perfect pitch – from drop shots plucked from the coaching manual with the dexterity and touch you would expect from a Stradivarius to those thunderous drives into the corners, struck with all the resonance of a big bass drum. Until that remarkable but unmistakable change in the whole complexion of the proceedings at the end of the third set, Edberg looked well beaten.

Two vital factors spurred him on, however – the thought of reaching his first Wimbledon final and the opportunity to achieve the greatest prize in any player's career, combined with the memory of his last confrontation with Mecir. That had been two months earlier in Norrkoping when Edberg, in what was said then to have been the most determined, fighting response of his career, recovered to beat Mecir from 1–4 in the fifth set of the decisive rubber, to sustain Sweden's hold on the Davis Cup.

'I had that Davis Cup match in mind even when I was 3–1 down in the fifth set this time,' said Edberg as he kept repeating, 'It's hard to believe I could come back from being so far down. I felt such a long way off after losing the first two sets. After he broke me at 4–4 in the first set, I didn't feel I could do anything. I didn't know what to do. Everything was very flat – but I stayed with him.'

Eyes front for members of the Committee of Management as Peter Jackson watches from behind (left to right) Mike Hann, former champion Virginia Wade and Geoff Brown.

There were two moments which could have been the points of no return for Edberg. The first came on the second break point in the seventh game of the third set, when Mecir, with the court at his mercy, played a backhand loosely into the net. The second came at 15–40, 3–4 for Edberg in the fourth set when he played a marvellous backhand volley.

In the final set, by which time Edberg had a noticeably sharper spring in his step and he could hardly wait for the next point to begin, he broke for 4–3 with a superb defensive lob and then a thrilling, lunging follow-up backhand volley. That certainly was the play of a potential champion. Yet the match finished on a quite bizarre point.

As Mecir played the lob which he felt sure would rescue him from Edberg's first match point, the Swede charged back, more in hope than expectation, and lashed a forehand which he did well even to direct into court. The momentum of that effort was still carrying Edberg into the back canvas as Mecir, with ample time and apparently amazed that the ball even came back, plopped a backhand volley softly into the net.

It was no wonder that a broad smile broke across Edberg's normally expressionless face, as he allowed himself to lean against and partly slip down the canvas before acknowledging his friends, especially coach Tony Pickard, in the players' box.

As Edberg went home that night, probably pinching himself to make sure that the events earlier in the day had not been just a fantasy, so Becker may have been doing the same, except in his case it would have been in disbelief that he too was not already in the final.

His match with Lendl had been stopped with Becker leading 6–4, 6–3, 6–7, but in the tie-break Becker was presented with three match points. The way he lost the first of them, at 6–4, could have haunted him for years had he failed to finish things off the next day. Perhaps he simply had too much time in which to play the shot. Perhaps he was over-confident and was already thinking, 'That's it, the match is over.' Neither he, nor the rest of us, will ever know. But instead of calmly putting away the sort of forehand volley he could almost have played with his eyes shut at any other time, he dumped it into the bottom of the net. 6–5!

Still it was match point but now with Lendl serving, and he promptly demonstrated how a forehand volley should be played. On Becker's third match point at 8–7, after Lendl had driven the first set point of his own wide at 7–6, a winning serve to the West German's backhand came to his rescue. Leading 9–8, Lendl, bravely masking the thigh strain which was becoming more and more of a handicap, especially when he served, opened up the court again with another formidable backhand return, and the Becker reply was easily tucked away. The former champion had lost not only three match points on top of five chances to break for 2–1 in that third set, but had conceded his first set in the fortnight.

For the ladies in waiting, Steffi Graf and Martina Navratilova, their principal duty on the eve of their women's singles final was to try and maintain their success in the doubles. For Miss Graf that meant little more than a comfortable work-out as she and Gabriela Sabatini won their way into the final of the women's doubles by beating Chris Evert and Wendy Turnbull, 6–3, 6–4, in just under an hour.

Miss Navratilova's working day was much longer than she would have desired. No sooner had she and Emilio Sanchez left Court 2, after a 6–4, 3–6, 6–3 victory over the unseeded Steve Kruger and Molly Van Nostrand in the mixed doubles, than they were back for a quarter-final against two Americans, Kelly Jones and Gretchen Magers, formerly Gretchen Rush. Rain intervened at 4–4 in the second set after Miss Navratilova and her partner had lost the first 7–6. Their opponents were keen to wait on that night in the hope of resuming, but she decided that the singles must come first and retired.

Back in the women's doubles the Russians, Larisa Savchenko and Natalia Zvereva, also reached the final, taking only 59 minutes to beat two Americans who had both done well in the singles, Katrina Adams and Zina Garrison, 6–3, 6–3.

John Fitzgerald and Anders Jarryd joined Ken Flach and Robert Seguso in the men's doubles final, but only after what developed into a tremendous tussle with Peter Doohan and Jim Grabb. They actually led 4–1 in the fourth set before the more experienced combination of Fitzgerald and Jarryd powered back in exhilarating style to win 7–6, 6–2, 1–6, 7–6. It had been quite a day – and the best of Wimbledon 1988 was still to come.

D A Y

12/13/14

Saturday 2 July

Sunday 3 July

Monday 4 July

Not for the first time in recent years, there was unfinished business to be dealt with before the stage could be set for the showpiece of the day, the final of the women's singles. Three years earlier, in 1985, Boris Becker had to complete a semi-final victory over Sweden's Anders Jarryd on the morning of the women's final. As that match carried him on to becoming, at 17, Wimbledon's youngest champion, he should have had no qualms this time about having to finish off the match against Ivan Lendl which he should have wrapped up the night before.

Although he eventually did so, 6–4, 6–3, 6–7, 6–4, Becker made desperately hard work of it and with two more rain breaks – one of 33 minutes, the other, after just two more minutes of play, for 37 minutes – meant they had taken two hours 11 minutes over the set.

It was amid mounting exasperation after he had seen five more match points, on top of the three the night before, elude him that Becker eventually drilled the ninth past a forlorn Lendl at the net. Throughout this section of the match Lendl wore a bandage heavily strapped round his strained thigh muscle, which clearly restricted his mobility, especially when it came to quick lateral movements. The injury also prevented him from sitting down at the change-overs. Lendl said that if he had not been at Wimbledon or some other Grand Slam final he would have defaulted.

The day's play was in three stages. In the first, they reached 2–2 in that fourth set, with Becker missing a point to go ahead 3–1 before a heavy shower stopped the already delayed play after 18 minutes. In part two, they had warmed up for five minutes and played one game, with Becker taking his aces count from seven to nine, before up went the umbrellas again.

It was during part three that Becker ran into trouble of an unexpected kind. The crowd laughed as he screamed with frustration and then buried his head into the back canvas after missing his sixth match point. Best of all, some of them thought it was a huge joke when, before allowing Lendl to serve to save match point number eight, Becker walked away and asked a lineswoman what shot he should try to play this time, bearing in mind that so many others had failed.

The debate which then raged was over whether Becker's actions were instinctive jokes or deliberate ploys to try and disrupt Lendl's concentration. If it was the latter, it certainly did not work, for Lendl immediately responded with one of the most fearsome serves he had produced in the match. Becker's comments later, in which he certainly implied that he did not see anything wrong with trying to distract opponents and cited several examples of other players doing the same, did not help and may even have explained why the greater weight of crowd support in the final was clearly with Stefan Edberg.

And for my next trick . . . Cristiano Caratti from Italy, another junior hoping to match Stefan Edberg's achievement in the future.

120

It was not until 3.38 pm that Martina Navratilova hit the first serve as she set out to try and make the record she currently shares with Helen Wills Moody all her own, with a ninth singles title. In the two hours 45 minutes which followed, including a 45-minute break for rain later in the final set, the significance of the £148,500 prize money was forgotten. Passion and power, constantly fuelled by pride, were all that mattered.

When Miss Navratilova led 2–0 in the second set, having recovered from 3–5 to take the first set during a spell in which Miss Graf forgot how much her backhand was supposed to have improved since last year, the celebration flags for the defending champion were at the ready. Yet at almost precisely that moment Miss Graf produced an astonishing burst of forceful, exemplary tennis and in a matter of minutes it became clear that Miss Navratilova's legendary reign was ending.

Later Miss Graf joined in the obvious mixture of sympathy and admiration for Miss Navratilova who, in athletics parlance, had been left standing in this long-distance race by her opponent's last lap from the bell. In Miss Graf's case, the warning bell rang in her head at 0–2 in the second set, at which point, significantly, she gave up the new racket she had been using and resorted to the slightly looser-strung one she had used in the semi-finals against Pam Shriver.

Two flashing service returns changed everything. They were both off the forehand, of course. During the nine whirlwind games which followed, breaking Miss Navratilova's heart, as well as ending her record of winning 47 consecutive singles matches, Miss Graf sustained a power and speed about the court probably unmatched even by the champion she was in the process of deposing.

Miss Graf swept from a stuttering first gear to top in a matter of seconds. One savage winner followed another, their impact biting into Miss Navratilova's mind as well as into those increasingly tiring muscles. To concede 12 years in a Wimbledon final is not to be recommended. The last eight minutes, following the rain stoppage immediately after Miss Navratilova had

A look of resignation from Ivan Lendl, with left thigh heavily bandaged, as he begins to realize his Wimbledon dreams are fading again.

struck two rousing backhands to break back to 1–3 in the final set, were the saddest.

The growing look of resignation, after she was immediately broken again and then served two successive double faults in the final game, told it all. As she said later, however, 'I'd have loved to break the record but eight ain't bad. Many people dream of just one, so I don't want to be too greedy.'

Miss Navratilova certainly accepted, with a champion's grace and realism, what must have been a cruel defeat to bear. 'I didn't succumb to any pressure, I succumbed to a better player,' she said, after what she called 'the end of a chapter', rather than the end of one era and the start of another, as many were suggesting.

Her only complaint, quite rightly, was against those few in the crowd who insensitively slow hand-clapped her during the transformation stage of the second set for taking extra seconds to wipe raindrops from her glasses. As for her thoughts on the new champion, Miss Navratilova said generously, 'Her speed is her biggest weapon. She not only reaches shots which most other players couldn't reach, but returns them as winners. And if she doesn't, she just whacks the big forehand. She has incredible spring in her step and is the fastest player I've ever met.'

As a final congratulatory gesture, Miss Navratilova later sought out Miss Graf, now needing only the US Open title to become only the third woman to achieve the Grand Slam, and presented her with the diamond-studded tennis racket brooch which boxer Sugar Ray Leonard had given her as a good luck charm. 'It deserves to be with a great new champion,' she said. Some lucky soul in the crowd went home with Miss Graf's racket, which she threw into the stand in her happiness at the end of the match.

It was a few minutes after 6 pm when the match finished. By the time the presentations, initial celebrations and interviews were over, it was too late for Miss Graf and Gabriela Sabatini to start the final of the women's doubles, especially as at 7.57 pm the fourth and final rain stoppage of the day left the men's doubles final still delicately balanced. Ken Flach and Robert Seguso were a set all and 5–4 up with serve in the third set, against second seeds John Fitzgerald and Anders Jarryd, when the covers went back on for the night.

By the following morning, the lowest depression over southern Britain at this time of year since 1956 was doing its worst – an infuriating steady drizzle, between heavier downpours. Hour after hour the crowds waited patiently for the 'brighter period' which the weathermen kept promising was on its way.

Then just as it looked as if there would be no play at all, for what would have been only the fourth time on a singles final day since The All England Club moved from Worple Road to Church Road in 1922, there was frantic activity as the clouds parted. More than four and a half hours late, at 6.33 pm, Edberg launched into his first service game with two mighty service winners and an ace. Becker, looking rattled, gathered only four points as Edberg moved to 3–0, with a point for 4–0, before Becker held on to his fifth game point and then broke back to love in the only bad game his opponent was to play on this momentous occasion. Then the rain re-started.

They had played for 23 minutes and Edberg was leading 3–2. At 7.33 pm came the inevitable announcement that play was abandoned, making this the first time that a men's singles final had stretched over from one day to the next.

The most unfortunate victims of the weather were undoubtedly Fitzgerald and Flach. Play in their match, which had been switched from Centre Court, the night before, to Court 1, lasted only another six minutes. Fitzgerald, a beaten finalist in this event with Pat Cash three years earlier, had the unenviable task of serving to save the third set, which they resumed at 4–5. At 0–30, while still trying to warm up, he double-faulted. Flach and Seguso grabbed the second of their set points as Seguso delivered a service return which landed right between the Australian and the Swede.

Meanwhile the final of the women's doubles was also restricted to two games. Miss Graf and Miss Sabatini reached 1–1 against the Soviet pair, Natalia Zvereva and Larisa Savchenko, for whom visa extensions were necessary, thanks to the British weather.

So into a third Monday, with ominous suggestions that a third Tuesday, Wednesday or Thursday might be necessary, if the worst of the weather predictions were to prove true. The hope had been for the Becker–Edberg clash to resume at 11 am. It was still raining! But at 12.56 pm about 11,000 spectators, who had managed to take an extra day off or find friends to use their tickets, welcomed the players back on court.

Becker quickly continued the recovery he had launched the previous evening by taking the set from 2–3 to 5–3, while Edberg, openly urging himself to 'concentrate', seemed to have endless problems with his service toss. With Becker ahead at 5–4, by which time they had played a further 16 minutes, there was yet more frustration caused by the rain. This time the break lasted one hour 40 minutes.

The former champion quickly held to 15, for the set, saved three break points, despite double-faulting twice, for 1–1 in the second and generally, at that stage, looked more likely to take control. Then came the vital seventh game of the set when Edberg double-faulted to 30–40, escaped luckily on his next serve and suddenly seemed to assume altogether fresh confidence.

Certainly from the start of the second set tie-break he steadily became more and more

dominant as a bemused Becker did not seem to know how to cope with a suddenly alien, threatening situation. Almost 23 hours after the match had first started Edberg, 22, barely given to more than a shy smile most of the time, was lying on the Centre Court, kicking his legs in the air to celebrate a magnificent triumph. Only 22 days after Becker had beaten him in the final at Queen's Club, Edberg had gained revenge in the sweetest possible manner, 4–6, 7–6, 6–4, 6–2.

Edberg, whose only previous match with Becker on grass had been a victory when they met in the junior boys' singles at Wimbledon in 1983, had played handsomely, as well as whole-heartedly, to become the first player from Sweden to hold the gleaming, golden trophy since Bjorn Borg, the man who inspired the present generation of his fellow countrymen, in 1980.

It was, as many observed, ample proof that 'the good guys can win'. It also put him in the same category as Borg and Rod Laver as the only players who have twice come back from being two sets down to win a Grand Slam title. He had also done so against Wally Masur on his way to winning the Australian Open for the first time.

Throughout those first two sets against Becker, both of which could have slipped away from him, Edberg always had in his mind his semi-final comeback from two sets down (and 1–3 in the fifth) against Mecir. Winning the second set tie-break 7–2 was the key for the detective's son. From then on it rapidly became 'the best match I've ever played in a Grand Slam tournament'.

By the end of the third set he could sense Becker becoming irritated and disillusioned, having collected a caution for racket abuse. That

Martina Navratilova's joy at taking the first set.

Steffi Graf strikes back.

The moment of victory.

'Bad luck,' says Tom Gullikson (left) after beating twin brother Tim, to retain the 35 and Over Men's Invitation Singles title.

lifted Edberg's confidence even more. He was a champion worth waiting for, and his success was a fitting reward for the work he and his coach Tony Pickard had put in since deciding the previous autumn to try and make 1988 Stefan's Wimbledon year.

An hour after the trophy was his, Edberg was still shaking his head and saying, 'It's hard to believe I've really won it; it hasn't sunk in yet.' He was just as surprised by the way Becker gave up the Championship point when, off an Edberg mis-hit, he buried a simple backhand volley in the net.

'He only had to play it back into court, but instead of trying to play the ball he went to hit it into my body,' said the new champion. 'It was a stupid thing to do. He didn't know what to do in the end. I didn't give him a chance.'

So true. As Becker kept telling us all along, these matches have little to do with tennis. They are won with the heart and the head. Becker, it seemed, had been more concerned about beating Pat Cash and Ivan Lendl.

Edberg and Becker closed the singles programme for another year, but while they were doing so Miss Graf was picking up her second title, as she and Miss Sabatini were taken to a long, tense and often thrilling third set, in which they saved two match points, before beating Miss Zvereva and Miss Savchenko 6–3, 1–6, 12–10. The final set alone took more than an hour and a half before it was Miss Zvereva's serve which was ultimately broken in the 22nd game.

Eventually, in a match which had started on Saturday and continued briefly on Sunday, Flach and Seguso retained their men's doubles crown, the first pair to do so since Peter Fleming and John McEnroe in 1984. They completed their 6–4, 2–6, 6–4, 7–6 victory in a fourth set tie-break, but only after all four players had been involved in a heated exchange over a net serve.

In both finals there was a break with tradition, with the President, HRH The Duke of Kent, watching the last moments of both the men's and women's doubles on Courts 1 and 2 respectively and then presenting the champions with their trophies there, as there was no chance to invite them to make the customary appearance to collect their trophies and take their bows in the Royal Box.

Fitzgerald, in particular, had a hectic final day for he also reached the semi-final of the mixed

doubles, in which defending champions Jeremy Bates and Jo Duric, the seventh seeds, had gone out in the second round. Fitzgerald and Liz Smylie were beaten by Sherwood Stewart and Zina Garrison, who went on to beat unseeded fellow Americans, 6–1, 7–6, in the final.

Sherwood, at 42, became the oldest mixed doubles champion and the oldest player to win one of the five major titles for the first time. Tom Gullikson, meanwhile, retained the 35 and Over Men's Invitation Singles, beating his brother Tim (coach to Martina Navratilova) 6–2, 7–6 in the final, after overcoming another of today's most prominent coaches, Tony Roche, in the semi-finals. The Gulliksons lost their 35 and Over Invitation Doubles title, however, when they were beaten in the first round by eventual champions, Bob Hewitt and Frew McMillan. They, in turn, overcame the event's most popular pair, Ken Rosewall and Fred Stolle, 6–4, 7–5 in the final.

In the junior singles the titles went, in both cases, to players from countries which had never enjoyed such success before. Nicolas Pereira, from Venezuela, runner-up in the French junior boys' event a month earlier, won the boys' title 7–6, 6–2 from Guillaume Raoux of France, after outstanding wins over two leading Australians, Jason Stoltenberg and Richard Fromberg, in his two previous rounds. Brenda Schultz, the tall, imposing and hard-hitting Dutch girl, already 46 in the women's world rankings, justified her top seeding in the girls' singles when she beat France's Emmanuelle Derly 7–6, 6–1 in the final.

Gretchen Magers won the Ladies' Plate when the 1987 winner, Sara Gomer, had to retire with an injury sustained while out jogging that morning. That left just the junior doubles events. Both titles went to Australians. Jo-Anne Faull and Rachel McQuillan won the girls' title, beating the strong French contenders Emmanuelle Derly and Alexia Dechaume in the final, while in the boys' event Jason Stoltenberg and Todd Woodbridge retained the title. It was almost 9 pm when they finished on Court 2, making Woodbridge not only one of the first to step out on court for Wimbledon 1988, having opened the Centre Court programme against Pat

Overleaf: A long wait for the men's singles final.

Cash, but also one of the last to leave.

The vile weather for so much of the last four days inevitably cast something of a pall over the closing stages of The Championships, especially as neither the players nor the spectators were able to sit back and enjoy the final matches, particularly in the doubles and the ancillary events.

It also meant that when The Champions' Dinner went ahead, as planned, at the Savoy on the second Sunday night, there was by then only one champion, Steffi Graf, to be toasted. Yet there was no doubt that Wimbledon eventually finished with two new, exciting, sporting champions, both of whom could go on to bring further distinction to the exclusive Roll of Honour they have now joined.

And if the rain had not intervened one could be fairly certain that Edberg would have stood up alongside Miss Graf at The Champions' Dinner and echoed her sentiments that winning Wimbledon was the greatest thrill of her career. From the huge grin which hardly left Edberg's face for hours after he became champion, everyone could see that was undoubtedly so.

On days like this you need a sense of humour.

Mental toughness helped Stefan Edberg earn the greatest victory of his career.

Boris reaches for a winner . . .

. . . but it is not enough.

Stefan Edberg emulates Bjorn Borg in victory and celebration.

Right: Steffi Graf dashes back to cover her partner, Gabriela Sabatini, on the way to winning her second title, in the women's doubles.

Umpire John Parry ponders what action to take as (left to right) Anders Jarryd, John Fitzgerald and Ken Flach have their say over a disputed call in the men's doubles final, while Robert Seguso simply waits for the verdict, before the Americans went on to retain the title.

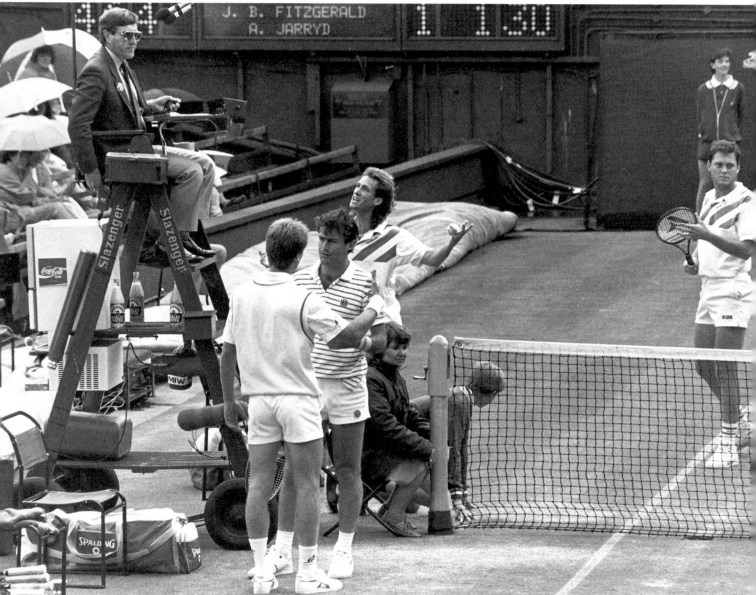

Stefan Edberg and Steffi Graf proudly display their trophies.

Ken Flach and Robert Seguso (top right) retain the men's doubles title.

Gabriela Sabatini and Steffi Graf after receiving the women's doubles trophy from (in the background) the President of The All England Club, HRH The Duke of Kent.

'We've done it.' Sherwood Stewart and Zina Garrison congratulate each other on winning the mixed doubles title.

The next generation (right) – Brenda Schultz of The Netherlands and Nicolas Pereira from Venezuela, the junior singles champions.

Tom Gullikson (right) retained the 35 and Over Men's Invitation Singles title.

140

The previous generation . . . Twenty-one years after winning the men's doubles crown for the first time, Frew McMillan (left) and Bob Hewitt celebrate the 35 and Over title.

Overleaf: Grand Slam champions Don Budge and Margaret Court join Steffi Graf, now three-quarters of the way towards a 1988 Grand Slam, at The Champions' Dinner.

CHAMPIONSHIP
RECORDS 1988

LIST OF COMPETITORS

LADIES

Adams, Miss K. (U.S.A.)
Antonoplis, Miss L. (U.S.A.)
Bakkum, Miss C. (Netherlands)
Balestrat, Mrs. C. M. (Australia)
Barg, Miss P. (U.S.A.)
Benjamin, Miss C. (U.S.A.)
Betzner, Miss A. (West Germany)
Bollegraf, Miss M. M. (Netherlands)
Bonsignori, Miss F. (Italy)
Budarova, Miss I. (Czechoslovakia)
Burgin, Miss E. M. (U.S.A.)
Bykova, Miss N. (U.S.S.R.)
Byrne, Miss J. M. (Australia)
Casals, Miss R. (U.S.A.)
Catlin, Miss T. A. (Great Britain)
Cioffi, Miss H. L. (U.S.A.)
Collins, Miss S. L. (U.S.A.)
Cordwell, Miss B. J. (New Zealand)
Cueto, Miss I. (West Germany)
Daniels, Mrs. P. F. (U.S.A.)
Dechaume, Miss A. (France)
Demongeot, Miss I. (France)
Derly, Miss E. (France)
Devries, Miss A. (Belgium)
Driehuis, Miss I. (Netherlands)
Durie, Miss J. M. (Great Britain)
Evert, Miss C. M. (U.S.A.)
Fairbank, Miss R. D. (U.S.A.)
Faull, Miss J.-A. (Australia)
Fendick, Miss P. A. (U.S.A.)
Fernandez, Miss A. M. (U.S.A.)
Fernandez, Miss G. (Puerto Rico)
Fernandez, Miss M. J. (U.S.A.)
Ferrando, Miss L. (Italy)
Field, Miss L. (Australia)
Foxworth, Miss K. (U.S.A.)
Frazier, Miss A. (U.S.A.)
Garrison, Miss Z. L. (U.S.A.)
Garrone, Miss L. (Italy)
Gerken, Miss B. S. (U.S.A.)
Godman, Miss S. (Great Britain)

Golarsa, Miss L. (Italy)
Goles, Miss S. (Yugoslavia)
Gomer, Miss S. L. (Great Britain)
Goodling, Miss J. E. (U.S.A.)
Gould, Miss L. C. (Great Britain)
Graf, Miss S. (West Germany)
Gregory, Miss L. (South Africa)
Grossman, Miss A. (U.S.A.)
Grunfeld, Miss A. L. (Great Britain)
Gurney, Miss M. L. (U.S.A.)
Hakami, Miss E. (U.S.A.)
Halard, Miss J. (France)
Hanika, Miss S. (West Germany)
Harper, Mrs. T. A. (U.S.A.)
Henricksson, Miss A. B. (U.S.A.)
Herr, Miss E. A. (U.S.A.)
Herreman, Miss N. (France)
Hetherington, Miss J. M. (Canada)
Holikova, Miss A. (Czechoslovakia)
Horvath, Miss E. K. (U.S.A.)
Hu, Miss Na (U.S.A.)
Hunter, Miss K. F. (Great Britain)
Hy, Miss P. (Hong Kong)
Inoue, Miss E. (Japan)
Jagerman, Miss N. A. M. (Netherlands)
Jaggard, Miss M. (Australia)
Javer, Miss M. A. (Great Britain)
Jolissaint, Miss C. (Switzerland)
Jones, Miss C. L. (U.S.A.)
Kaplan, Miss J. C. (U.S.A.)
Kelesi, Miss H. (Canada)
Kijimuta, Miss A. (Japan)
Koizumi, Miss Y. (Japan)
Krapl, Miss E. (Switzerland)
Kuczynska, Miss I. (Poland)
Lake, Miss V. (Great Britain)
Lapi, Miss L. (Italy)
Lindqvist, Miss C. (Sweden)
Lindstrom, Miss M. (Sweden)
Loosemore, Miss S. J. (Great Britain)
Ludloff, Miss H. A. (U.S.A.)

MacGregor, Miss C. (U.S.A.)
MacGregor, Miss C. B. (U.S.A.)
Magers, Mrs. S. W. (U.S.A.)
Maleeva, Miss K. (Bulgaria)
Maleeva, Miss M. (Bulgaria)
Mandlikova, Mrs. H. (Australia)
McNeil, Miss L. M. (U.S.A.)
McQuillan, Miss R. (Australia)
Medrado, Miss P. S. (Brazil)
Medvedeva, Miss N. (U.S.S.R.)
Meier, Miss S. (West Germany)
Mesker, Miss M. A. (Netherlands)
Meskhi, Miss L. G. (U.S.S.R.)
Minter, Miss A. L. (Australia)
Minter, Miss E. A. (Australia)
Miro, Miss G. (Brazil)
Morton, Miss T. (Australia)
Nagelsen. Miss B. (U.S.A.)
Navratilova, Miss M. (U.S.A.)
Niepel, Miss A. M. (Great Britain)
Novotna, Miss J. (Czechoslovakia)
O'Neill, Miss L. (Australia)
Okamoto, Miss K. (Japan)
Paradis, Miss P. (France)
Parkhomenko, Mrs. S. (U.S.S.R.)
Pete, Mrs. M. H. (U.S.A.)
Pfaff, Miss E. S. (West Germany)
Phelps, Miss T. (U.S.A.)
Porwik, Miss C. (West Germany)
Potter, Miss B. C. (U.S.A.)
Probst, Miss W. (West Germany)
Provis, Miss N. (Australia)
Quentrec, Miss K. (France)
Rehe, Miss S. C. (U.S.A.)
Reinach, Miss E. (South Africa)
Reis, Miss R. (U.S.A.)
Reynolds, Miss C. S. (U.S.A.)
Richardson, Miss J. A. (New Zealand)
Romano, Miss B. (Italy)
Russell, Miss J. C. (U.S.A.)
Sabatini, Miss G. (Argentina)

Salmon, Miss J. A. (Great Britain)
Sanchez, Miss A. (Spain)
Sato, Miss N. (Japan)
Savchenko, Miss L. (U.S.S.R.)
Scheuer-Larsen, Miss T. (Denmark)
Schimper, Mrs. K. T. (South Africa)
Schultz, Miss B. (Netherlands)
Scott, Miss A. (Australia)
Seguso, Mrs. C. K. (Canada)
Shriver, Miss P. H. (U.S.A.)
Simpkin, Miss A. (Great Britain)
Singer, Miss C. (West Germany)
Sloane, Miss S. P. (U.S.A.)
Smith, Miss P. G. (U.S.A.)
Smoller, Miss J. (U.S.A.)
Smylie, Mrs. P. D. (Australia)
Spadea, Miss L. (U.S.A.)
Stafford, Miss S. (U.S.A.)
Steinmetz, Miss K. A. (U.S.A.)
Suire, Miss C. (France)
Sukova, Miss H. (Czechoslovakia)
Tacon, Miss J. M. (Great Britain)
Tanvier, Miss C. (France)
Tauziat, Miss N. (France)
Thompson, Miss J. G. (Australia)
Turnbull, Miss W. M. (Australia)
Van Nostrand, Miss M. (U.S.A.)
Van Rensburg, Miss D. S. (South Africa)
Villagran, Miss A. C. (Argentina)
Wasserman, Miss S. (Belgium)
Werdel, Miss R. M. (U.S.A.)
White, Miss R. M. (U.S.A.)
White, Miss W. E. (U.S.A.)
Wiesner, Mrs. H. W. (Austria)
Witvoet, Miss H. (Netherlands)
Wood, Miss C. J. (Great Britain)
Wood, Miss M. (U.S.A.)
Yanagi, Miss M. (Japan)
Zrubakova, Miss R. (Czechoslovakia)
Zvereva, Miss N. (U.S.S.R.)

GENTLEMEN

Acuna, R. (Chile)
Aldrich, P. (South Africa)
Ali, Z. (India)
Anger, M. W. (U.S.A.)
Annacone, P. (U.S.A.)
Antonitsch, A. (Austria)
Arraya, P. (Peru)
Bahrami, M. (Iran)
Bailey, C. A. (Great Britain)
Barbosa, G. (Brazil)
Barr, S. (Australia)
Basham, M. (Australia)
Bates, M. J. (Great Britain)
Bauer, M. (U.S.A.)
Becker, B. (West Germany)
Beckman, C. (U.S.A.)
Benhabiles, T. (France)
Berger, J. (U.S.A.)
Bergstrom, C. (Sweden)
Birner, S. (Czechoslovakia)
Bloom, G. (Israel)
Botfield, S. (Great Britain)
Brice, A. (Great Britain)
Broad, N. (South Africa)
Cahill, D. (Australia)
Camporese, O. (Italy)
Cancellotti, F. (Italy)
Cane, P. (Italy)
Carter, P. (Australia)
Casal, S. (Spain)
Cash, P. (Australia)
Castle, A. N. (Great Britain)
Chamberlin, P. (U.S.A.)
Champion, T. (France)
Chang, M. (U.S.A.)
Chesnokov, A. (U.S.S.R.)
Cihak, J. (Czechoslovakia)
Connell, G. (Canada)
Connors, J. S. (U.S.A.)
Cox, C. H. (U.S.A.)
Curren, K. (U.S.A.)
Davis, M. (U.S.A.)
Davis, S. E. (U.S.A.)
De La Pena, H. (Argentina)
Denton, S. (U.S.A.)
Depalmer, M. (U.S.A.)
Devries, S. (U.S.A.)
Donnelly, G. (U.S.A.)
Doohan, P. (Australia)

Doumbia, Y. (Senegal)
Dowlen, D. (U.S.A.)
Drewett, B. D. (Australia)
Dyke, B. (Australia)
Edberg, S. (Sweden)
Edwards, E. (South Africa)
Evernden, K. (New Zealand)
Fancutt, M. T. (Australia)
Felgate, D. C. (Great Britain)
Ferreira, M. (India)
Fichardt, G. (South Africa)
Fitzgerald, J. B. (Australia)
Flach, K. (U.S.A.)
Fleming, P. (U.S.A.)
Flur, M. (U.S.A.)
Forget, G. (France)
Frana, J. (Argentina)
Frawley, J. (Australia)
Freeman, M. (U.S.A.)
Fulwood, N. A. (Great Britain)
Giammalva, S. (U.S.A.)
Goldie, D. (U.S.A.)
Goodall, J. M. (Great Britain)
Grabb, J. (U.S.A.)
Green, W. B. (South Africa)
Guenthardt, H. P. (Switzerland)
Gunnarsson, J. (Sweden)
Gustafsson, M. (Sweden)
Hlasek, J. (Switzerland)
Holmes, G. (U.S.A.)
Hooper, C. (U.S.A.)
Hoysted, P. (Australia)
Ivanisevic, G. (Yugoslavia)
Jarryd, A. (Sweden)
Jelen, E. (West Germany)
Jensen, L. B. (U.S.A.)
Jones, K. (U.S.A.)
Kohlberg, A. (U.S.A.)
Korda, P. (Czechoslovakia)
Korita, E. (U.S.A.)
Kriek, J. C. (U.S.A.)
Krishnan, R. (India)
Kroon, N. (Sweden)
Kruger, S. (South Africa)
Kuhnen, P. (West Germany)
Laurendeau, M. (Canada)
Lavalle, L. (Mexico)
Layendecker, G. (U.S.A.)
Leach, R. (U.S.A.)

Leconte, H. (France)
Lendl, I. (Czechoslovakia)
Levine, B. H. (South Africa)
Limberger, C. A. (Australia)
Lindgren, P. (Sweden)
Lloyd, J. M. (Great Britain)
Lopez-Maeso, J. (Spain)
Luna, F. (Spain)
Lundgren, P. (Sweden)
MacPherson, D. (Australia)
Mansdorf, A. (Israel)
Marcelino, D. (Brazil)
Masso, E. (Argentina)
Masur, W. (Australia)
Matuszewski, R. (U.S.A.)
Mayotte, T. S. (U.S.A.)
McEnroe, J. P. (U.S.A.)
Mecir, M. (Czechoslovakia)
Medem, S. (West Germany)
Meinecke, T. (West Germany)
Menezes, M. (Brazil)
Michibata, G. (Canada)
Miller, C. D. (U.S.A.)
Moir, B. N. (South Africa)
Moraing, H. (West Germany)
Moraing, P. (West Germany)
Moreno, A. (Mexico)
Mortensen, M. (Denmark)
Muller, G. (South Africa)
Narducci, M. (Italy)
Nargiso, D. (Italy)
Navratil, J. (Czechoslovakia)
Nelson, T. (U.S.A.)
Nijssen, T. (Netherlands)
Novacek, K. (Czechoslovakia)
Nystrom, J. (Sweden)
Odizor, N. (Nigeria)
Olkhovsky, A. (U.S.S.R.)
Oosting, H. (Netherlands)
Osterthun, R. (West Germany)
Palandjian, P. (U.S.A.)
Pate, D. (U.S.A.)
Pawsat, T. (U.S.A.)
Pernfors, M. (Sweden)
Petchey, M. R. J. (Great Britain)
Pimek, L. (Czechoslovakia)
Potier, L. (France)
Pridham, C. (Canada)
Pugh, J. (U.S.A.)

Purcell, M. (U.S.A.)
Rahnasto, O. (Finland)
Reneberg, R. A. (U.S.A.)
Riglewski, U. (West Germany)
Ross, J. (U.S.A.)
Rostagno, D. (U.S.A.)
Saceanu, C. (West Germany)
Sanchez, E. (Spain)
Sanchez, J. (Spain)
Scanlon, W. (U.S.A.)
Schapers, M. (Netherlands)
Scott, L. (U.S.A.)
Seguso, R. (U.S.A.)
Shaw, S. M. (Great Britain)
Shiras, L. (U.S.A.)
Siegel, T. (U.S.A.)
Skoff, H. (Austria)
Slozil, P. (Czechoslovakia)
Smid, T. (Czechoslovakia)
Smith, R. (Bahamas)
Srejber, M. (Czechoslovakia)
Stankovic, B. (Czechoslovakia)
Steeb, C.-U. (West Germany)
Stenlund, U. (Sweden)
Stewart, S. E. (U.S.A.)
Stoltenberg, J. (Australia)
Svantesson, T. (Sweden)
Svensson, J. B. (Sweden)
Taroczy, B. (Hungary)
Tideman, M. (Sweden)
Van Boeckel, H. P. (Netherlands)
Van Rensburg, C. J. (South Africa)
Van't Hof, R. W. (U.S.A.)
Visser, D. T. (South Africa)
Volkov, A. (U.S.S.R.)
Walker, M. T. (Great Britain)
Warder, L. (Australia)
Warwick, K. (Australia)
Whichello, R. A. W. (Great Britain)
Wilander, M. (Sweden)
Wilkison, T. (U.S.A.)
Winogradsky, E. (France)
Woodbridge, T. (Australia)
Woodforde, M. (Australia)
Youl, S. (Australia)
Yzaga, J. (Peru)
Zivojinovic, S. (Yugoslavia)

MAIDEN NAMES OF LADY COMPETITORS

Mrs. C. M. Balestrat—Miss D. L. Fromholtz   Mrs. P. F. Daniels—Miss M. L. Piatek

Mrs. T. A. Harper—Miss M. Louie   Mrs. S. W. Magers—Miss G. A. Rush   Mrs. H. Mandlikova—Miss H. Mandlikova

Mrs. S. Parkhomenko—Miss S. Cherneva   Mrs. M. H. Pete—Miss S. A. Walsh   Mrs. C. K. Seguso—Miss C. K. Bassett

Mrs. P. D. Smylie—Miss E. M. Sayers   Mrs. H. W. Wiesner—Miss J. Polzl

EVENT I.—THE GENTLEMEN'S SINGLES CHAMPIONSHIP

Holder: P. CASH

The Winner will become the holder, for the year only, of the CHALLENGE CUP presented to the Club by KING GEORGE V, and also of the CHALLENGE CUP presented by The All England Lawn Tennis and Croquet Club. The First Prize is a piece of silver, known as "The Renshaw Cup" annually presented to the Club by the surviving members of the family of the late ERNEST and WILLIAM RENSHAW. The Winner will receive silver replicas of the two Challenge Cups. A personal prize and a Silver Medal will be presented to the Runner-up and a Bronze Medal to each defeated Semi-finalist. Details of Prize Money will be found on page 17.

FIRST ROUND

1	**I. Lendl** ①	(CZ.)
2	D. C. Felgate	(G.B.) (W)
3	G. Muller	(S.A.)
4	D. Cahill	(A.)
5	P. Lundgren	(SW.)
6	N. Kroon	(SW.)
7	A. Antonitsch	(AU.)
8	M. Schapers	(NTH.)
9	G. Connell	(C.)
10	R. Krishnan	(IN.)
11	J. C. Kriek	(U.S.A.)
12	M. Woodforde	(A.)
13	D. Nargiso	(IT.) (Q)
14	J. M. Goodall	(G.B.) (W)
15	G. Ivanisevic	(YU.) (Q)
16	**A. Mansdorf** ⑮	(ISR.)
17	**T. S. Mayotte** ⑩	(U.S.A.)
18	M. W. Anger	(U.S.A.)
19	G. Holmes	(U.S.A.)
20	N. A. Fulwood	(G.B.) (W)
21	J. Nystrom	(SW.)
22	J. Pugh	(U.S.A.)
23	J. Gunnarsson	(SW.)
24	C. A. Bailey	(G.B.) (W)
25	B. N. Moir	(S.A.) (Q)
26	S. Casal	(SP.)
27	M. R. J. Petchey	(G.B.) (W)
28	H. Moraing	(W.G.) (Q)
29	G. Layendecker	(U.S.A.)
30	M. Chang	(U.S.A.)
31	T. Svantesson	(SW.) (Q)
32	**H. Leconte** ⑦	(F.)
33	**P. Cash** ④	(A.)
34	T. Woodbridge	(A.)
35	J. Frana	(ARG.)
36	W. Scanlon	(U.S.A.) (Q)
37	F. Cancellotti	(IT.)
38	J. B. Fitzgerald	(A.)
39	L. Pimek	(CZ.)
40	C. Bergstrom	(SW.)
41	A. Olkhovsky	(U.S.S.R.) (Q)
42	T. Smid	(CZ.)
43	P. Aldrich	(S.A.)
44	P. Arraya	(PE.)
45	C. Pridham	(C.)
46	G. Fichardt	(S.A.) (Q)
47	U. Riglewski	(W.G.)
48	**A. Chesnokov** ⑭	(U.S.S.R.)
49	**J. B. Svensson** ⑫	(SW.)
50	T. Wilkison	(U.S.A.)
51	T. Benhabiles	(F.)
52	M. Gustafsson	(SW.)
53	B. Stankovic	(CZ.)
54	T. Nelson	(U.S.A.)
55	P. Annacone	(U.S.A.)
56	M. Laurendeau	(C.) (L)
57	S. Giammalva	(U.S.A.)
58	R. Osterthun	(W.G.)
59	M. Srejber	(CZ.)
60	N. Odizor	(NI.) (L)
61	K. Novacek	(CZ.)
62	P. Lindgren	(SW.)
63	J. Frawley	(A.)
64	**B. Becker** ⑥	(W.G.)
65	**J. S. Connors** ⑤	(U.S.A.)
66	L. Shiras	(U.S.A.)
67	J. Stoltenberg	(A.) (Q)
68	Y. Doumbia	(SEN.)
69	J. Yzaga	(PE.)
70	D. Rostagno	(U.S.A.)
71	M. Davis	(U.S.A.)
72	B. Dyke	(A.)
73	D. Goldie	(U.S.A.)
74	J. Hlasek	(SWZ.)
75	P. Kuhnen	(W.G.)
76	H. P. Van Boeckel	(NTH.) (Q)
77	J. Grabb	(U.S.A.)
78	J. Cihak	(CZ.)
79	T. Nijssen	(NTH.)
80	**A. Jarryd** ⑪	(SW.)
81	**E. Sanchez** ⑬	(SP.)
82	J. Sanchez	(SP.)
83	M. Narducci	(IT.)
84	P. Korda	(CZ.)
85	J. Navratil	(CZ.)
86	S. Botfield	(G.B.) (W)
87	C.-U. Steeb	(W.G.)
88	S. Youl	(A.)
89	P. Doohan	(A.)
90	K. Flach	(U.S.A.)
91	J. Berger	(U.S.A.)
92	F. Luna	(SP.)
93	C. Saceanu	(W.G.)
94	R. A. Reneberg	(U.S.A.)
95	G. Forget	(F.)
96	**S. Edberg** ③	(SW.)
97	**J. P. McEnroe** ⑧	(U.S.A.)
98	H. Skoff	(AU.)
99	S. M. Shaw	(G.B.) (W)
100	W. Masur	(A.)
101	M. J. Bates	(G.B.)
102	C. J. Van Rensburg	(S.A.)
103	R. Seguso	(U.S.A.)
104	S. Barr	(A.) (Q)
105	D. Pate	(U.S.A.)
106	U. Stenlund	(SW.)
107	K. Curren	(U.S.A.)
108	R. Acuna	(CH.) (Q)
109	A. Volkov	(U.S.S.R.)
110	T. Champion	(F.)
111	A. Moreno	(M.)
112	**M. Mecir** ⑨	(CZ.)
113	**S. Zivojinovic** ⑯	(YU.)
114	H. De La Pena	(ARG.)
115	J. Ross	(U.S.A.)
116	P. Cane	(IT.)
117	R. A. W. Whichello	(G.B.) (W)
118	T. Meinecke	(W.G.)
119	E. Jelen	(W.G.)
120	G. Bloom	(ISR.)
121	K. Evernden	(N.Z.)
122	J. Potier	(F.)
123	M. Oosting	(NTH.)
124	C. A. Limberger	(A.) (Q)
125	A. N. Castle	(G.B.) (Q)
126	G. Michibata	(C.)
127	E. Masso	(ARG.)
128	**M. Wilander** ②	(SW.)

SECOND ROUND

- I. Lendl — 6-4, 6-1, 6-3
- D. Cahill — 6-7, 6-2, 6-2, 6-0
- P. Lundgren — 4-6, 4-6, 6-4, 7-6, 6-0
- M. Schapers — 4-6, 6-4, 6-4, 7-6
- R. Krishnan — 6-2, 6-4, 5-7, 1-6, 7-5
- M. Woodforde — 7-6, 6-3, 6-4
- D. Nargiso — 6-2, 6-3, 7-6
- A. Mansdorf ⑮ — 6-3, 6-2, 1-6, 6-1
- T. S. Mayotte ⑩ — 6-4, 6-4, 6-3
- G. Holmes — 6-3, 3-6, 6-1, 6-3
- J. Nystrom — 2-6, 6-4, 6-4, 6-3
- J. Gunnarsson — 6-3, 7-6, 6-4
- B. N. Moir — 6-2, 6-3, 4-6, 6-1
- H. Moraing — 6-3, 7-5, 6-4
- M. Chang — 7-5, 1-6, 6-4, 6-2
- H. Leconte ⑦ — 6-4, 6-2, 6-2
- P. Cash ④ — 6-1, 6-1, 6-2
- J. Frana — 4-6, 3-6, 6-3, 6-3, 6-2
- J. B. Fitzgerald — 6-3, 3-6, 6-1, 6-4
- C. Bergstrom — 6-1, 6-4, 6-1
- A. Olkhovsky — 6-4, 6-4, 6-4
- P. Aldrich — 6-7, 6-4, 6-4, 4-6, 6-2
- C. Pridham — 6-3, 6-4, 6-4
- U. Riglewski — 7-5, 6-4, 6-4
- J. B. Svensson ⑫ — 6-1, 7-6, 6-3
- M. Gustafsson — 6-3, 6-4, 6-4
- B. Stankovic — 6-3, 2-6, 6-3, 6-4
- P. Annacone — 6-0, 6-2, 6-3
- S. Giammalva — 6-7, 6-1, 6-2, 1-6, 6-3
- M. Srejber — 6-3, 7-6, 4-6, 6-3
- K. Novacek — 6-2, 6-4, 7-6
- B. Becker ⑥ — 6-3, 6-1, 6-2
- J. S. Connors ⑤ — 6-3, 7-6, 6-1
- J. Stoltenberg — 6-4, 6-4, 6-3
- D. Rostagno — 6-0, 6-3, 7-5
- M. Davis — 5-7, 7-5, 7-6, 7-5
- J. Hlasek — 6-3, 4-6, 6-4, 7-5
- P. Kuhnen — 6-3, 6-2, 6-4
- J. Grabb — 6-0, 6-3, 6-4
- A. Jarryd ⑪ — 6-2, 6-0, 6-2
- E. Sanchez ⑬ — 6-3, 6-3, 6-4
- P. Korda — 6-3, 3-6, 6-3, 6-2
- S. Botfield — 6-4, 6-4, 6-3
- S. Youl — 2-6, 6-3, 4-6, 6-2, 6-4
- K. Flach — 7-5, 7-6, 6-3
- J. Berger — 6-1, 7-6, 6-0
- R. A. Reneberg — 7-5, 2-6, 6-3, 7-5
- S. Edberg ③ — 6-4, 3-6, 6-3, 6-4
- J. P. McEnroe ⑧ — 6-1, 7-5, 6-1
- W. Masur — 7-5, 7-6, 4-6, 6-1
- M. J. Bates — 2-6, 1-6, 6-3, 7-5, 6-4
- R. Seguso — 6-7, 6-3, 6-2, 6-4
- D. Pate — 6-2, 6-3, 6-7, 6-2
- R. Acuna — 7-6, 6-7, 6-4, 6-4
- A. Volkov — 4-6, 7-6, 3-6, 6-4, 6-2
- M. Mecir ⑨ — 7-6, 7-6, 6-2
- S. Zivojinovic ⑯ — 5-7, 7-6, 6-4, 6-4
- J. Ross — 6-7, 6-2, 6-1, 3-6, 6-1
- T. Meinecke — 5-7, 7-6, 7-5, 6-2
- E. Jelen — 6-3, 3-6, 6-4, 6-3
- K. Evernden — 7-6, 6-4, 6-2
- M. Oosting — 7-5, 6-1, 6-3
- G. Michibata — 6-4, 7-5, 6-4
- M. Wilander ② — 6-3, 6-4, 7-6

THIRD ROUND

- I. Lendl ① — 5-7, 6-2, 6-4, 6-4
- M. Schapers — 7-5, 6-2, 6-2
- M. Woodforde — 6-7, 6-4, 6-3, 6-3
- D. Nargiso — 6-3, 3-0, ret'd
- T. S. Mayotte ⑩ — 6-3, 6-3, 6-4
- J. Nystrom — 6-4, 3-6, 6-3, 6-7, 6-1
- B. N. Moir — 7-6, 6-3, 4-6, 6-3
- H. Leconte ⑦ — 2-6, 7-6, 6-2, 6-3
- P. Cash ④ — 6-2, 4-6, 6-1, 6-4
- J. B. Fitzgerald — 6-4, 4-6, 7-5, 6-3
- A. Olkhovsky — 6-4, 6-4, 6-2
- C. Pridham — 6-7, 7-5, 6-3, 7-5
- J. B. Svensson ⑫ — 6-1, 6-2, 6-4
- P. Annacone — 6-4, 6-2, 6-4
- S. Giammalva — 1-6, 6-1, 6-2, 1-6, 6-3
- B. Becker ⑥ — 6-3, 6-4, 6-4
- J. S. Connors ⑤ — 7-6, 6-2, 6-4
- D. Rostagno — 6-2, 6-3, 6-7, 4-6, 16-14
- P. Kuhnen — 7-6, 5-7, 4-6, 6-1, 6-4
- J. Grabb — 3-6, 7-6, 6-3, 6-0
- P. Korda — 7-6, 6-3, 3-6, 0-6, 6-1
- S. Youl — 6-2, 6-3, 6-4
- K. Flach — 7-5, 6-1, 6-4
- S. Edberg ③ — 6-3, 7-6, 5-7, 6-2
- W. Masur — 7-5, 7-6, 6-3
- R. Seguso — 6-7, 6-3, 6-2, 6-4
- R. Acuna — 3-6, 5-7, 7-6, 7-6, 6-4
- M. Mecir ⑨ — 6-2, 6-4, 6-4
- S. Zivojinovic ⑯ — 6-4, 6-4, 6-4
- E. Jelen — 6-1, 6-1, 6-4
- M. Oosting — 4-6, 7-6, 6-4, 3-6, 6-1
- M. Wilander ② — 6-2, 7-6, 6-4

FOURTH ROUND

- I. Lendl ① — 6-7, 7-6, 6-4, 6-7, 6-1
- M. Woodforde — 6-3, 6-4, 6-3
- T. S. Mayotte ⑩ — 6-4, 4-6, 6-2, 6-4
- H. Leconte ⑦ — 3-6, 6-1, 7-6, 6-1
- P. Cash ④ — 6-1, 6-2, 6-4
- A. Olkhovsky — 3-6, 6-3, 6-4, 6-3
- P. Annacone — 6-4, 2-6, 3-6, 6-4
- B. Becker ⑥ — 7-6, 6-4, 6-4
- J. S. Connors ⑤ — 7-5, 4-6, 4-6, 6-2, 7-5
- P. Kuhnen — 6-1, 6-4, 6-4
- S. Youl — 6-4, 7-6, 6-0
- S. Edberg ③ — 6-2, 7-5, 2-6, 7-5
- W. Masur — 6-4, 6-4, 6-7, 6-1
- M. Mecir ⑨ — 6-3, 6-4, 6-2
- S. Zivojinovic ⑯ — 3-6, 6-3, 7-6, 6-3
- M. Wilander ② — 6-1, 6-4, 6-4

QUARTER-FINALS

- I. Lendl ① — 7-5, 6-7 (6-8), 6-7 (4-7), 7-5, 10-8
- T. S. Mayotte ⑩ — 6-4, 7-6 (7-5), 4-6, 6-2
- P. Cash ④ — 6-3, 6-3, 6-3
- B. Becker ⑥ — 6-3, 6-4, 6-4
- P. Kuhnen — 5-7, 7-6 (9-7), 7-6 (7-2), 6-7 (4-7), 6-3
- S. Edberg ③ — 6-2, 6-4, 6-4
- M. Mecir ⑨ — 4-6, 6-2, 6-4, 6-2
- M. Wilander ② — 6-4, 7-6 (7-1), 7-5

SEMI-FINALS

- I. Lendl ① — 7-6 (7-2), 7-6 (7-1), 6-3
- B. Becker ⑥ — 6-4, 6-3, 6-4
- S. Edberg ③ — 6-3, 4-6, 6-1, 7-6 (7-2)
- M. Mecir ⑨ — 6-3, 6-1, 6-3

FINAL

- B. Becker ⑥ — 6-4, 6-3, 6-7 (8-10), 6-4
- S. Edberg ③ — 4-6, 2-6, 6-4, 6-3, 6-4

CHAMPION

S. Edberg ③ — 4-6, 7-6 (7-2), 6-4, 6-2

Heavy type denotes seeded players. The encircled figure against names denotes the order in which they have been seeded. (W) Wild card. (Q) Qualifier. (L) Lucky loser. The Matches will be the best of five sets.
For particulars of Abbreviations, see page 43.

EVENT II.—THE GENTLEMEN'S DOUBLES CHAMPIONSHIP

Holders: K. FLACH and R. SEGUSO

The Winners will become the holders, for the year only, of the CHALLENGE CUPS, presented by the OXFORD UNIVERSITY LAWN TENNIS CLUB and the late SIR HERBERT WILBERFORCE respectively. The Winners will receive silver replicas of the Challenge Cups. A personal prize and a Silver Medal will be presented to each of the Runners-up, and a Bronze Medal to each defeated Semi-finalist. Details of Prize Money will be found on page 17.

FIRST ROUND	SECOND ROUND	THIRD ROUND	QUARTER-FINALS	SEMI-FINALS	FINAL
1 K. Flach and R. Seguso ①	K. Flach and R. Seguso ① 6–2, 7–6, 6–3	K. Flach and R. Seguso ① 6–7, 7–6, 6–3, 6–4	K. Flach and R. Seguso ① 7–6 (7–3), 6–1, 7–6 (7–4)	K. Flach and R. Seguso ① 4–6, 6–3, 6–4, 7–6 (8–6), 7–5, 6–2	
2 S. Birner and J. Navratil					
3 T. Pawsat and T. Svantesson	T. Pawsat and T. Svantesson 7–6, 7–6, 1–6, 2–6, 6–3				
4 C. A. Limberger and M. Schapers					
5 J. Frana and J. Lopez-Maeso	A. Olkhovsky and A. Volkov 6–2, 6–2, 7–6	B. Dyke and T. Nijssen ⑮ 7–6, 6–7, 7–6, 6–4			
(W) 6 A. Olkhovsky and A. Volkov					
(Q) 7 M. Basham and L. B. Jensen					
8 B. Dyke and T. Nijssen ⑮	B. Dyke and T. Nijssen ⑮ 7–6, 6–4, 3–6, 7–6				
9 W. Masur and M. Woodforde ⑩	W. Masur and M. Woodforde ⑩ 6–2, 3–6, 6–3, 6–4	W. Masur and M. Woodforde ⑩ 6–2, 6–4, 7–6	W. Masur and M. Woodforde ⑩ 7–6 (7–1), 6–3, 6–2		
10 M. Gustafsson and M. Purcell					
11 L. Warder and S. Youl	L. Warder and S. Youl 6–2, 6–3, 6–2				
(L) 12 A. Brice and J. M. Goodall					
13 J. Ross and K. Warwick	J. M. Lloyd and S. M. Shaw 7–6, 6–3, 7–6	J. M. Lloyd and S. M. Shaw 6–4, 6–4, 7–5			
(W) 14 J. M. Lloyd and S. M. Shaw					
15 T. Meinecke and R. Osterthun	P. Annacone and C. J. Van Rensburg ⑦ 6–1, 3–6, 7–6, 6–4				
16 P. Annacone and C. J. Van Rensburg ⑦					
17 S. Casal and E. Sanchez ③	S. Casal and E. Sanchez ③ 6–0, 6–1, 6–4	M. W. Anger and G. Holmes 6–1, 6–4, 6–4	E. Edwards and G. Muller 7–6 (7–5), 6–3, 7–6 (9–7)	E. Edwards and G. Muller 7–6 (7–2), 3–6, 7–6 (11–9), 6–4	
18 H. Moraing and P. Moraing					
(Q) 19 T. Champion and E. Winogradsky	M. W. Anger and G. Holmes 7–6, 4–0, ret'd				
20 M. W. Anger and G. Holmes					
(W) 21 H. P. Guenthardt and B. Taroczy	E. Korita and N. Odizor 7–5, 4–6, 6–7, 6–2, 6–4	E. Edwards and G. Muller 3–6, 7–6, 7–6, 6–7, 6–4			
22 E. Korita and N. Odizor					
23 E. Edwards and G. Muller	E. Edwards and G. Muller 7–6, 4–6, 6–4, 7–5				
24 A. Kohlberg and R. W. Van 't Hof ⑭					
25 P. Aldrich and D. T. Visser ⑫	P. Aldrich and D. T. Visser ⑫ 7–6, 7–6, 6–4	P. Aldrich and D. T. Visser ⑫ 7–6, 6–1	P. Aldrich and D. T. Visser ⑫ 7–6 (7–1), 4–6, 7–6 (7–4), 1–6, 10–8		
26 D. Dowlen and M. Freeman					
(Q) 27 S. Medem and O. Rahnasto	S. Medem and O. Rahnasto 6–4, 7–5, 1–6, 6–7, 6–2				
28 P. Carter and P. Lundgren					
(Q) 29 S. Devries and R. Matuszewski	M. Flur and T. Siegel 3–6, 2–6, 6–3, 6–4, 6–4	R. Leach and J. Pugh ⑥ 6–0, 6–4, 2–6, 7–5			
30 M. Flur and T. Siegel					
31 L. Lavalle and J. Sanchez	R. Leach and J. Pugh ⑥ 7–5, 7–6, 6–4				
32 R. Leach and J. Pugh ⑥					
33 G. Forget and T. Smid ⑤	G. Forget and T. Smid ⑤ 3–6, 7–6, 6–4, 3–6, 6–4	G. Forget and T. Smid ⑤ 7–6, 4–6, 6–4, 3–6, 6–3	G. Forget and T. Smid ⑤ 7–6 (7–2), 6–1, 6–2	P. Doohan and J. Grabb 6–4, 7–6 (7–3), 7–6 (10–8)	J. B. Fitzgerald and A. Jarryd ② 7–6 (7–5), 6–2, 1–6, 7–6 (7–3)
34 J. Gunnarsson and N. Kroon					
35 C. Hooper and T. Nelson	N. Broad and S. Kruger 6–4, 7–6, 6–1				
(Q) 36 N. Broad and S. Kruger					
37 J. B. Svensson and M. Tideman	D. C. Felgate and N. A. Fulwood 3–6, 3–6, 6–2, 6–3, 9–7	M. Depalmer and G. Donnelly 6–3, 7–6, 3–6, 6–4			
(W) 38 D. C. Felgate and N. A. Fulwood					
39 M. Depalmer and G. Donnelly	M. Depalmer and G. Donnelly 6–4, 6–3, 6–4				
40 M. Davis and B. D. Drewett ⑪					
(L) 41 G. Barbosa and M. Menezes	Z. Ali and M. Ferreira 6–2, 6–3, 6–4	S. E. Davis and D. Goldie 6–4, 6–3, 6–2	P. Doohan and J. Grabb w/o		
(L) 42 Z. Ali and M. Ferreira					
43 J. Cihak and K. Novacek	S. E. Davis and D. Goldie 7–5, 5–7, 7–6, 6–4				
44 S. E. Davis and D. Goldie					
45 D. MacPherson and H. P. Van Boeckel	P. Doohan and J. Grabb 7–5, 7–6, 6–7, 7–6	P. Doohan and J. Grabb 6–3, 6–2, 7–6			
46 P. Doohan and J. Grabb					
47 P. Chamberlin and L. Scott	P. Chamberlin and L. Scott 5–7, 6–4, 6–2, 6–4				
(L) 48 B. H. Levine and P. Palandjian					
49 K. Evernden and J. C. Kriek ⑧	K. Evernden and J. C. Kriek ⑧ 6–7, 6–4, 6–2, 4–6, 7–6	K. Evernden and J. C. Kriek ⑧ 7–5, 6–4, 6–4	K. Evernden and J. C. Kriek ⑧ 2–6, 6–2, 7–5, 7–6 (7–3)	J. B. Fitzgerald and A. Jarryd ② 4–6, 6–3, 6–4	
50 S. Giammalva and R. A. Reneberg					
51 S. Denton and S. E. Stewart	S. Denton and S. E. Stewart 4–6, 6–3, 7–5, 6–7, 6–4				
52 R. Acuna and D. Marcelino					
53 E. Jelen and P. Kuhnen	E. Jelen and P. Kuhnen 3–6, 7–6, 6–3, 7–6	E. Jelen and P. Kuhnen 6–2, 7–5, 6–7, 6–4			
54 C. Beckman and G. Layendecker					
55 O. Camporese and D. Nargiso	D. Cahill and S. Zivojinovic ⑨ 4–6, 6–3, 6–0, 7–6				
56 D. Cahill and S. Zivojinovic ⑨					
57 M. J. Bates and P. Lundgren ⑯	M. J. Bates and P. Lundgren ⑯ 6–4, 6–2, 7–5	G. Connell and G. Michibata 6–3, 6–4, 6–4	J. B. Fitzgerald and A. Jarryd ② 6–4, 6–4, 7–6 (7–3)		
(W) 58 C. A. Bailey and M. R. J. Petchey					
59 G. Connell and G. Michibata	G. Connell and G. Michibata 7–6, 6–3, 6–7, 4–6, 8–6				
60 J. Stoltenberg and T. Woodbridge					
61 M. Bahrami and M. Mortensen	M. Bahrami and M. Mortensen 7–6, 6–4, 7–5	J. B. Fitzgerald and A. Jarryd ② 6–1, 6–2, 6–1			
62 K. Jones and R. Smith					
63 P. Cane and P. Korda	J. B. Fitzgerald and A. Jarryd ② 6–3, 3–6, 6–0, 6–3				
64 J. B. Fitzgerald and A. Jarryd ②					

Heavy type denotes seeded players. The encircled figure against names denotes the order in which they have been seeded. (W) = Wild cards. (Q) = Qualifiers. (L) = Lucky losers. The Matches will be the best of five sets.

146

EVENT III.—THE LADIES' SINGLES CHAMPIONSHIP

Holder: Miss M. NAVRATILOVA

The Winner will become the holder, for the year only, of the CHALLENGE TROPHY presented by The All England Lawn Tennis and Croquet Club. The Winner will receive a silver replica of the Trophy. A personal prize and a Silver Medal will be presented to the Runner-up and a Bronze Medal to each defeated Semi-finalist. Details of Prize Money will be found on page 17.

FIRST ROUND

1 Miss S. Graf ① (W.G.)
2 Miss Na Hu (U.S.A.)
(L) 3 Miss K. Quentrec (F.)
4 Miss J. Halard (F.)
(W) 5 Mrs. T. A. Harper (U.S.A.)
6 Miss S. J. Loosemore (G.B.)
7 Miss T. Phelps (U.S.A.)
8 Miss W. M. Turnbull (A.)
9 Miss I. Kuczynska (POL.)
10 Miss B. Nagelsen (U.S.A.)
11 Miss E. S. Pfaff (W.G.)
(Q) 12 Miss L. Field (A.)
(Q) 13 Miss S. L. Collins (U.S.A.)
14 Miss L. G. Meskhi (U.S.S.R.)
15 Miss N. A. M. Jagerman (NTH.)
16 Miss M. J. Fernandez ⑯ (U.S.A.)
17 Mrs. H. Mandlikova ⑨ (A.)
18 Miss L. Garrone (IT.)
19 Miss A. B. Henricksson (U.S.A.)
20 Miss E. A. Herr (U.S.A.)
21 Miss M. M. Bollegraf (NTH.)
22 Miss B. Romano (IT.)
23 Miss A. L. Minter (A.)
24 Miss A. Holikova (CZ.)
25 Mrs. H. W. Wiesner (AU.)
26 Miss L. Golarsa (IT.)
27 Miss R. M. White (U.S.A.)
(W) 28 Miss C. J. Wood (G.B.)
29 Miss N. Herreman (F.)
30 Mrs. M. H. Pete (U.S.A.)
31 Miss P. Paradis (F.)
32 Miss M. Maleeva ⑦ (BUL.)
33 Miss P. H. Shriver ③ (U.S.A.)
34 Miss D. S. Van Rensburg (S.A.)
35 Miss J. M. Hetherington (C.)
36 Mrs. S. Parkhomenko (U.S.S.R.)
37 Miss C. Porwik (W.G.)
(L) 38 Miss L. O'Neill (A.)
39 Miss C. Suire (F.)
40 Miss S. C. Rehe (U.S.A.)
41 Miss M. A. Javer (G.B.)
42 Miss S. Meier (W.G.)
43 Miss B. J. Cordwell (N.Z.)
44 Miss E. M. Burgin (U.S.A.)
(W) 45 Miss L. C. Gould (G.B.)
46 Miss I. Cueto (W.G.)
(W) 47 Miss A. Simpkin (G.B.)
48 Miss K. Maleeva ⑭ (BUL.)
49 Miss Z. L. Garrison ⑫ (U.S.A.)
50 Miss W. E. White (U.S.A.)
51 Miss F. Bonsignori (IT.)
52 Mrs. C. M. Balestrat (A.)
53 Miss G. Fernandez (P.R.)
54 Miss B. Schultz (NTH.)
55 Miss A. Frazier (U.S.A.)
56 Miss E. A. Minter (A.)
57 Miss C. Tanvier (F.)
58 Miss P. S. Medrado (BR.)
(W) 59 Miss A. L. Grunfeld (G.B.)
60 Miss M. L. Gurney (U.S.A.)
61 Miss R. Zrubakova (CZ.)
62 Miss H. A. Ludloff (U.S.A.)
63 Mrs. C. K. Seguso (C.)
64 Miss G. Sabatini ⑤ (ARG.)
65 Miss H. Sukova ⑥ (CZ.)
66 Miss I. Demongeot (F.)
67 Miss J. Novotna (CZ.)
68 Miss T. Scheuer-Larsen (D.)
69 Miss E. Inoue (J.)
70 Miss W. Probst (W.G.)
(Q) 71 Miss P. Barg (U.S.A.)
72 Miss S. L. Gomer (G.B.)
73 Miss E. Krapl (SWZ.)
74 Miss N. Bykova (U.S.S.R.)
75 Miss B. C. Potter (U.S.A.)
76 Miss L. Lapi (IT.)
77 Miss M. Lindstrom (SW.)
(Q) 78 Miss J.-A. Faull (A.)
79 Miss I. Budarova (CZ.)
(L) 80 Miss S. Stafford (U.S.A.)
81 Miss S. Hanika ⑮ (W.G.)
82 Miss H. L. Cioffi (U.S.A.)
83 Miss M. Jaggard (A.)
84 Miss H. Witvoet (NTH.)
(W) 85 Miss V. Lake (G.B.)
86 Miss K. Adams (U.S.A.)
87 Miss N. Tauziat (F.)
88 Miss A. Devries (B.)
89 Miss A. Sanchez (SP.)
(Q) 90 Miss K. Okamoto (J.)
91 Miss G. Miro (BR.)
92 Miss A. Kijimuta (J.)
93 Miss C. Singer (W.G.)
94 Miss S. Wasserman (B.)
95 Miss A. Dechaume (F.)
96 Miss C. M. Evert ④ (U.S.A.)
97 Miss N. Zvereva ⑧ (U.S.S.R.)
(Q) 98 Miss N. Reis (U.S.A.)
99 Miss P. A. Fendick (U.S.A.)
100 Miss C. Benjamin (U.S.A.)
101 Miss C. Jolissaint (SWZ.)
(Q) 102 Miss C. Gregory (S.A.)
103 Miss C. Lindqvist (SW.)
104 Miss E. Reinach (S.A.)
105 Miss J. M. Durie (G.B.)
106 Miss M. Werdel (U.S.A.)
107 Miss R. D. Fairbank (U.S.A.)
108 Mrs. P. F. Daniels (U.S.A.)
109 Miss S. P. Sloane (U.S.A.)
(W) 110 Miss T. A. Catlin (G.B.)
111 Miss N. Provis (A.)
112 Miss L. M. McNeil ⑩ (U.S.A.)
113 Miss L. Savchenko ⑬ (U.S.S.R.)
114 Miss J. M. Byrne (A.)
115 Miss M. Yanagi (J.)
116 Miss B. S. Gerken (U.S.A.)
117 Miss A. C. Villagran (ARG.)
118 Miss L. Ferrando (IT.)
119 Mrs. P. D. Smylie (A.)
(W) 120 Miss J. A. Salmon (G.B.)
121 Mrs. S. W. Magers (U.S.A.)
122 Miss N. Kelesi (C.)
(Q) 123 Miss K. F. Hunter (G.B.)
124 Miss K. T. Schimper (S.A.)
125 Miss E. K. Horvath (U.S.A.)
126 Miss E. Hakami (U.S.A.)
127 Miss S. Goles (YU.)
128 Miss M. Navratilova ② (U.S.A.)

SECOND ROUND

Miss S. Graf ① 6-0, 6-0
Miss K. Quentrec 7-6, 6-1
Miss S. J. Loosemore 6-7, 6-3, 6-4
Miss T. Phelps 7-5, 6-7, 6-0
Miss I. Kuczynska 5-7, 6-1, 6-3
Miss L. Field 7-5, 6-3
Miss L. G. Meskhi 6-4, 4-6, 9-7
Miss M. J. Fernandez ⑯ 6-3, 6-2
Mrs. H. Mandlikova ⑨ 6-3, 7-5
Miss A. B. Henricksson 6-3, 6-2
Miss M. M. Bollegraf 6-1, 6-4
Miss A. L. Minter 6-3, 6-0
Miss L. Golarsa 6-3, 5-7, 6-3
Miss R. M. White 3-6, 6-3, 6-3
Miss N. Herreman 6-2, 6-2
Miss P. Paradis 6-4, 6-3
Miss P. H. Shriver ③ 6-2, 4-6, 8-6
Mrs. S. Parkhomenko 4-6, 6-4, 6-3
Miss L. O'Neill 7-5, 6-4
Miss S. C. Rehe 6-3, 5-7, 6-4
Miss S. Meier 2-6, 6-3, 9-7
Miss B. J. Cordwell 6-4, 6-3
Miss I. Cueto 7-6, 6-2
Miss K. Maleeva ⑭ 6-1, 6-0
Miss Z. L. Garrison ⑫ 6-3, 6-1
Mrs. C. M. Balestrat 6-7, 6-3, 6-0
Miss G. Fernandez 2-6, 6-4, 8-6
Miss E. A. Minter 7-5, 6-4
Miss C. Tanvier 6-3, 6-1
Miss M. L. Gurney 6-4, 7-5
Miss R. Zrubakova 6-3, 7-6
Miss G. Sabatini ⑤ 6-2, 6-2
Miss H. Sukova ⑥ 7-5, 1-6, 6-2
Miss J. Novotna 6-3, 7-5
Miss E. Inoue 5-7, 7-5, 6-2
Miss S. L. Gomer 7-6, 6-4
Miss N. Bykova 6-3, 3-6, 6-3
Miss B. C. Potter 6-3, 7-6
Miss J.-A. Faull 7-6, 6-3
Miss I. Budarova 7-6, 6-3
Miss S. Hanika ⑮ 6-1, 6-2
Miss H. Witvoet 6-2, 6-2
Miss K. Adams 6-3, 6-2
Miss N. Tauziat 6-2, 6-4
Miss K. Okamoto 6-3, 6-1
Miss A. Kijimuta 4-6, 6-0, 6-2
Miss C. Singer 6-4, 6-0
Miss C. M. Evert ④ 6-1, 6-2
Miss N. Zvereva ⑧ 6-2, 6-3
Miss P. A. Fendick 6-2, 6-3
Miss C. Jolissaint 6-7, 6-4, 6-3
Miss E. Reinach 7-6, 6-4
Miss J. M. Durie 6-4, 6-2
Miss R. D. Fairbank 6-2, 6-3
Miss S. P. Sloane 6-3, 6-1
Miss L. M. McNeil ⑩ 6-3, 7-5
Miss L. Savchenko ⑬ 6-2, 6-2
Miss M. Yanagi 6-4, 6-1
Miss A. C. Villagran 6-3, 6-3
Miss J. A. Salmon 6-4, 6-4
Mrs. S. W. Magers 7-6, 3-6, 7-5
Miss K. T. Schimper 6-4, 7-6
Miss E. Hakami 6-4, 6-4
Miss M. Navratilova ② 6-2, 6-1

THIRD ROUND

Miss S. Graf ① 6-2, 6-0
Miss T. Phelps 6-1, 6-1
Miss I. Kuczynska 7-5, 6-4
Miss M. J. Fernandez ⑯ 6-1, 7-5
Miss H. Mandlikova ⑨ 6-4, 6-2
Miss A. L. Minter 6-2, 6-2
Miss R. M. White 6-2, 6-2
Miss P. Paradis 6-4, 3-6, 8-6
Miss P. H. Shriver ③ 6-3, 6-4
Miss S. C. Rehe 4-6, 6-1, 6-4
Miss B. J. Cordwell 6-1, 5-7, 6-4
Miss K. Maleeva ⑭ 6-0, 6-4
Miss Z. L. Garrison ⑫ 6-4, 6-3
Miss E. A. Minter 6-3, 3-6, 6-2
Miss C. Tanvier 6-3, 6-3
Miss G. Sabatini ⑤ 6-4, 6-3
Miss H. Sukova ⑥ 6-2, 6-2
Miss E. Inoue 6-4, 6-2
Miss B. C. Potter 2-6, 6-4, 9-7
Miss J.-A. Faull 5-7, 6-1, 6-4
Miss S. Hanika ⑮ 6-1, 6-3
Miss K. Adams 2-6, 6-4, 6-4
Miss A. Kijimuta 7-5, 6-3
Miss C. M. Evert ④ 6-4, 3-6, 6-3
Miss N. Zvereva ⑧ 6-3, 6-3
Miss E. Reinach 6-1, 6-4
Miss R. D. Fairbank 6-2, 1-6, 7-5
Miss L. M. McNeil ⑩ 6-7, 6-4, 6-4
Miss L. Savchenko ⑬ 7-6, 6-3
Miss J. A. Salmon 6-7, 6-1, 6-2
Miss K. T. Schimper 6-4, 7-6
Miss M. Navratilova ② 6-2, 6-1

FOURTH ROUND

Miss S. Graf ① 6-3, 6-1
Miss M. J. Fernandez ⑯ 6-4, 6-1
Miss A. L. Minter 6-4, 6-3
Miss P. Paradis 6-4, 3-6, 9-7
Miss P. H. Shriver ③ 7-6, 7-6
Miss K. Maleeva ⑭ 6-0, 6-0
Miss Z. L. Garrison ⑫ 7-6, 6-0
Miss G. Sabatini ⑤ 6-2, 6-3
Miss H. Sukova ⑥ 6-7, 6-3, 6-2
Miss B. C. Potter 4-6, 6-3, 6-4
Miss K. Adams 6-3, 6-3
Miss C. M. Evert ④ 6-4, 6-0
Miss N. Zvereva ⑧ 6-2, 7-6
Miss R. D. Fairbank 7-6, 6-4
Miss L. Savchenko ⑬ 6-1, 6-2
Miss M. Navratilova ② 6-0, 6-4

QUARTER-FINALS

Miss S. Graf ① 6-2, 6-2
Miss P. Paradis 6-3, 5-7, 6-4
Miss P. H. Shriver ③ 6-2, 6-2
Miss Z. L. Garrison ⑫ 6-1, 3-6, 6-2
Miss H. Sukova ⑥ 7-6(7-4), 6-4
Miss C. M. Evert ④ 5-7, 6-3, 6-0
Miss R. D. Fairbank 6-2, 6-4
Miss M. Navratilova ② 6-4, 6-2

SEMI-FINALS

Miss S. Graf ① 6-3, 6-1
Miss P. H. Shriver ③ 6-4, 6-4
Miss C. M. Evert ④ 6-3, 7-6(7-4)
Miss M. Navratilova ② 4-6, 6-4, 7-5

Miss S. Graf ① 6-1, 6-2
Miss M. Navratilova ② 6-1, 4-6, 7-5

FINAL

Miss S. Graf ① 5-7, 6-2, 6-1

Heavy type denotes seeded players. The encircled figure against names denotes the order in which they have been seeded. (W) = Wild card. (Q) = Qualifier. (L) = Lucky loser. The Matches will be the best of three sets.
Maiden Names of Competitors will be found on page 44. For particulars of Abbreviations, see page 43.

EVENT IV.—THE LADIES' DOUBLES CHAMPIONSHIP

Holders: Miss C. KOHDE-KILSCH and Miss H. SUKOVA

The Winners will become the holders, for the year, of the CHALLENGE CUP presented by H.R.H. PRINCESS MARINA, DUCHESS OF KENT, the late President of The All England Lawn Tennis and Croquet Club. The Winners will receive silver replicas of the Challenge Cup. A personal prize and a Silver Medal will be presented to each of the Runners-up and a Bronze Medal to each defeated Semi-finalist. Details of Prize Money will be found on page 17.

	FIRST ROUND	SECOND ROUND	THIRD ROUND	QUARTER-FINALS	SEMI-FINALS	FINAL
1	Miss M. Navratilova and Miss P. H. Shriver ①	Miss M. Navratilova and Miss P. H. Shriver ① 6–2, 6–2	Miss M. Navratilova and Miss P. H. Shriver ① 6–4, 3–6, 7–5			
2	Miss L. Gregory and Miss R. Reis					
3	Miss J. E. Goodling and Miss C. L. Jones	Miss J. M. Byrne and Miss J. G. Thompson 7–6, 6–4				
4	Miss J. M. Byrne and Miss J. G. Thompson					
5	Mrs. C. M. Balestrat and Miss M. Maleeva	Miss L. Antonoplis and Miss B. S Gerken 6–1, 6–4	Miss L. Savchenko and Miss N. Zvereva ⑪ 6–2, 6–1			
6	Miss L. Antonoplis and Miss B. S. Gerken					
(Q) 7	Miss Y. Koizumi and Miss K. A. Steinmetz	Miss L. Savchenko and Miss N. Zvereva ⑪ 6–1, 6–4		Miss L. Savchenko and Miss N. Zvereva ⑪ 7–6 (7–3), 6–2		
8	Miss L. Savchenko and Miss N. Zvereva ⑪					
9	Miss C. Lindqvist and Miss T. Scheuer-Larsen ⑮	Miss C. Lindqvist and Miss T. Scheuer-Larsen ⑮ 7–5, 6–3	Miss C. Lindqvist and Miss T. Scheuer-Larsen ⑮ 6–4, 4–6, 6–2			
10	Miss B. J. Cordwell and Miss M. Van Nostrand					
11	Miss C. S. Reynolds and Miss P. G. Smith	Miss C. S. Reynolds and Miss P. G. Smith 6–2, 6–4				
12	Miss G. Miro and Miss A. C. Villagran					
13	Miss W. Probst and Miss A. Sanchez	Miss I. Driehuis and Miss M. A. Mesker 6–3, 6–4	Miss R. D. Fairbank and Miss G. Fernandez ⑨ 6–2, 6–3			
14	Miss I. Driehuis and Miss M. A. Mesker					
(L) 15	Miss L. O'Neill and Miss J. Smoller	Miss R. D. Fairbank and Miss G. Fernandez ⑨ 6–2. 3–6, 6–2		Miss R. D. Fairbank and Miss G. Fernandez ⑨ 6–0, 0–1, ret'd		
16	Miss R. D. Fairbank and Miss G. Fernandez ⑨					
17	Miss L. M. McNeil and Miss B. Nagelsen ④	Miss L. M. McNeil and Miss B. Nagelsen ④ 6–7, 6–3, 6–4	Miss L. M. McNeil and Miss B. Nagelsen ④ 3–6, 6–4, 6–3			
18	Miss N. Herreman and Miss P. Paradis					
19	Miss A. B. Henricksson and Miss C. Jolissaint	Miss A. B. Henricksson and Miss C. Jolissaint 6–4, 6–0				
20	Miss E. Hakami and Miss J. C. Kaplan					
21	Miss A. Devries and Miss S. Wasserman	Miss A. Devries and Miss S. Wasserman 7–5, 6–3	Miss J. M. Durie and Mrs. M. H. Pete ⑭ 6–4, 6–4, 6–3			
22	Miss A. Betzner and Mrs. H. W. Wiesner					
23	Miss C. MacGregor and Miss C. B. MacGregor	Miss J. M. Durie and Mrs. M. H. Pete ⑭ 7–5, 3–6, 6–4		Miss L. M. McNeil and Miss B. Nagelsen ④ 7–5, 3–6, 6–3		
24	Miss J. M. Durie and Mrs. M. H. Pete ⑭					
25	Miss M. M. Bollegraf and Miss N. Provis ⑰	Miss M. M. Bollegraf and Miss N. Provis ⑰ 2–6, 7–6, 6–3	Miss M. M. Bollegraf and Miss N. Provis ⑰ 6–4, 6–1			
26	Miss P. A. Fendick and Miss J. M. Hetherington					
27	Miss S. L. Collins and Miss Na Hu	Miss S. L. Collins and Miss Na Hu 7–5, 6–4				
28	Miss I. Budarova and Miss C. Singer					
29	Miss C. Benjamin and Miss A. Scott	Miss C. Benjamin and Miss A. Scott 6–2, 7–6	Miss K. Adams and Miss Z. L. Garrison ⑧ 6–2, 6–2			
(W) 30	Miss A. Simpkin and Miss J. M. Tacon					
(W) 31	Miss S. Godman and Miss A. M. Niepel	Miss K. Adams and Miss Z. L. Garrison ⑧ 6–0, 6–1		Miss K. Adams and Miss Z. L. Garrison ⑧ 6–1, 6–0		
32	Miss K. Adams and Miss Z. L. Garrison ⑧					
33	Miss E. M. Burgin and Miss R. M. White ⑦	Miss A. Dechaume and Miss E. Derly 6–4, 6–2	Miss A. Dechaume and Miss E. Derly 6–1, 6–3			
(Q) 34	Miss A. Dechaume and Miss E. Derly					
35	Miss E. K. Horvath and Miss M. Jaggard	Miss E. K. Horvath and Miss M. Jaggard 5–7, 6–3, 6–2				
36	Miss A. Frazier and Miss L. Spadea					
(L) 37	Miss A. Grossman and Miss M. Yanagi	Miss M. Lindstrom and Miss C. Porwik 6–1, 6–4	Miss M. Lindstrom and Miss C. Porwik 7–6, 2–6, 7–5			
38	Miss M. Lindstrom and Miss C. Porwik					
39	Mrs. T. A. Harper and Miss H. A. Ludloff	Mrs. H. Mandlikova and Miss B. C. Potter ⑫ 6–3, 6–4		Miss M. Lindstrom and Miss C. Porwik 6–0, 6–2		
40	Mrs. H. Mandlikova and Miss B. C. Potter ⑫					
41	Miss C. M. Evert and Miss W. M. Turnbull ⑬	Miss C. M. Evert and Miss W. M. Turnbull ⑬ 7–6, 4–6, 6–2	Miss C. M. Evert and Miss W. M. Turnbull ⑬ 7–6 (7–5), 6–7 (4–7), 7–5			
42	Miss N. Bykova and Miss N. Medvedeva					
43	Miss N. A. M. Jagerman and Miss S. C. Rehe	Miss N. A. M. Jagerman and Miss S. C. Rehe 6–4, 6–1		Miss C. M. Evert and Miss W. M. Turnbull ⑬ 0–6, 7–6 (7–3), 6–1		
44	Miss K. Okamoto and Mrs. P. H. Sato					
45	Miss H. Kelesi and Miss C. Tanvier	Miss H. Kelesi and Miss C. Tanvier 6–2, 6–1	Miss J. Novotna and Miss C. Suire 7–5, 2–6, 6–1			
46	Miss P. Barg and Mrs. P. F. Daniels					
47	Miss C. Bakkum and Miss B. Schultz	Miss J. Novotna and Miss C. Suire ⑤ 6–3, 6–4				
48	Miss J. Novotna and Miss C. Suire ⑤					
49	Miss E. S. Pfaff and Mrs. P. D. Smylie ⑥	Miss E. S. Pfaff and Mrs. P. D. Smylie ⑥ 5–7, 6–3, 6–2	Miss E. S. Pfaff and Mrs. P. D. Smylie ⑥ 6–7, 6–2, 6–4			
50	Miss R. Casals and Miss J. C. Russell					
51	Miss K. T. Schimper and Miss W. Wood	Mrs. S. W. Magers and Miss W. E. White 5–7, 7–6, 6–2		Miss E. S. Pfaff and Mrs. P. D. Smylie ⑥ 6–2, 6–3		
52	Mrs. S. W. Magers and Miss W. E. White					
(Q) 53	Miss J.-A. Faull and Miss R. McQuillan	Miss J.-A. Faull and Miss R. McQuillan 2–6, 6–4, 6–4	Miss I. Demongeot and Miss N. Tauziat ⑯ 6–2, 7–5			
54	Miss P. Hy and Miss D. S. Van Rensburg					
(W) 55	Miss V. Lake and Miss C. J. Wood	Miss I. Demongeot and Miss N. Tauziat ⑯ 3–6, 6–4, 6–1				
56	Miss I. Demongeot and Miss N. Tauziat ⑯					
57	Miss L. G. Meskhi and Mrs. S. Parkhomenko ⑩	Miss L. G. Meskhi and Mrs. S. Parkhomenko ⑩	Miss E. A. Herr and Miss K. Maleeva 6–4, 4–6, 7–6			
(W) 58	Miss S. L. Gomer and Miss J. A. Salmon					
59	Miss E. A. Herr and Miss K. Maleeva	Miss E. A. Herr and Miss K. Maleeva 6–3, 7–5		Miss S. Graf and Miss G. Sabatini ③ 6–3, 6–3		
(Q) 60	Miss L. Field and Miss E. Krapl					
61	Miss A. L. Minter and Miss H. Witvoet	Miss A. L. Minter and Miss H. Witvoet 6–0, 6–3	Miss S. Graf and Miss G. Sabatini ③ 7–6, 4–6, 7–5			
62	Miss A. M. Fernandez and Miss J. A. Richardson					
63	Miss I. Cueto and Miss P. S. Medrado	Miss S. Graf and Miss G. Sabatini ③ 6–1, 6–2				
64	Miss S. Graf and Miss G. Sabatini ③					

Quarter-finals / Semi-finals / Final results:

Miss L. Savchenko and Miss N. Zvereva ⑪ 6–4, 6–2 (vs Fairbank/Fernandez)

Miss K. Adams and Miss Z. L. Garrison ⑧ 6–4, 6–3 (vs McNeil/Nagelsen)

Miss C. M. Evert and Miss W. M. Turnbull ⑬ 3–6, 7–5, 6–2 (vs Lindstrom/Porwik)

Miss S. Graf and Miss G. Sabatini ③ 7–6 (7–4), 5–7, 8–6 (vs Pfaff/Smylie)

Miss L. Savchenko and Miss N. Zvereva ⑪ 6–3, 6–3 (Semi-final, vs Adams/Garrison)

Miss S. Graf and Miss G. Sabatini ③ 6–3, 6–4 (Semi-final, vs Evert/Turnbull)

Miss S. Graf and Miss G. Sabatini ③ 6–3, 1–6, 12–10 (Final)

Heavy type denotes seeded players. The encircled figure against names denotes the order in which they have been seeded. (W) = Wild cards. (Q) = Qualifiers. (L) = Lucky losers. The Matches will be the best of three sets. Maiden Names of Competitors will be found on page 44.

EVENT V.—THE MIXED DOUBLES CHAMPIONSHIP Holders: M. J. BATES and Miss J. M. DURIE

The Winners will become the holders, for the year, of the CHALLENGE CUP presented by the family of the late Mr. S. H. SMITH. The Winners will receive silver replicas of the Challenge Cup. A personal prize and a Silver Medal will be presented to each of the Runners-up and a Bronze Medal to each defeated Semi-finalist. Details of Prize Money will be found on page 17.

FIRST ROUND

1 **E. Sanchez and Miss M. Navratilova** ①
2 L. Shiras and Miss S. C. Rehe
3 P. Aldrich and Miss L. Gregory
4 S. Denton and Miss B. Schultz
5 B. Dyke and Miss J. C. Kaplan
(L) 6 G. Layendecker and Miss S. Stafford
(L) 7 S. Kruger and Miss M. Van Nostrand
8 **T. Nijssen and Miss M. M. Bollegraf** ⑫
9 **M. Mortensen and Miss T. Scheuer-Larsen** ⑬
(L)10 P. Hoystead and Miss T. Morton
(Q)11 C. D. Miller and Miss J. Smoller
12 K. Evernden and Miss J. A. Richardson
13 C. A. Limberger and Miss A. Scott
14 D. MacPherson and Miss J. M. Byrne
15 K. Jones and Mrs. S. W. Magers
16 **J. Grabb and Miss E. M. Burgin** ⑧
17 **J. Pugh and Miss J. Novotna** ③
18 W. B. Green and Miss D. S. Van Rensburg
19 M. Schapers and Miss A. B. Henricksson
20 E. Korita and Miss P. Barg
21 A. Kohlberg and Mrs. C. M. Balestrat
22 P. Carter and Miss C. Bakkum
23 L. Scott and Miss B. C. Potter
24 **R. Leach and Miss P. A. Fendick** ⑩
25 **M. Freeman and Miss L. M. McNeil** ⑯
26 N. Odizor and Miss C. S. Reynolds
27 C. Beckman and Miss C. Benjamin
28 M. Davis and Miss T. Phelps
29 M. Woodforde and Miss M. Jaggard
30 G. Connell and Miss H. Kelesi
(W)31 N. A. Fulwood and Miss J. A. Salmon
32 **C. J. Van Rensburg and Mrs. H. Mandlikova** ⑤
33 **M. J. Bates and Miss J. M. Durie** ⑦
34 A. N. Castle and Miss C. Suire
35 L. Warder and Miss C. Porwik
36 E. Edwards and Miss E. Reinach
37 M. Bauer and Miss E. S. Pfaff
38 R. Acuna and Miss J. M. Hetherington
39 M. T. Fancutt and Miss R. Casals
40 **S. E. Stewart and Miss Z. L. Garrison** ⑭
41 **D. Cahill and Miss N. Provis** ⑪
42 T. Nelson and Mrs. R. M. White
43 P. Chamberlin and Miss P. Hy
44 M. Tideman and Miss L. Field
45 D. Marcelino and Miss G. Miro
46 B. H. Levine and Miss R. Reis
47 T. Woodbridge and Miss H. Witvoet
48 **P. Annacone and Miss B. Nagelsen** ④
49 **D. T. Visser and Miss R. D. Fairbank** ⑥
(W)50 K. Flach and Mrs. C. K. Seguso
(W)51 J. M. Lloyd and Miss W. M. Turnbull
(W)52 S. M. Shaw and Miss C. Lindqvist
53 J. Sanchez and Miss A. Sanchez
54 T. Pawsat and Miss E. A. Herr
(L)55 M. T. Walker and Miss J. M. Tacon
(W)56 **P. Slozil and Miss S. Graf** ⑨
57 **R. W. Van't Hof and Mrs. P. F. Daniels** ⑮
58 S. Youl and Miss A. L. Minter
(Q)59 R. Smith and Miss K. Foxworth
(W)60 C. A. Bailey and Miss T. A. Catlin
(Q)61 S. Barr and Miss S. L. Collins
62 C. Hooper and Miss P. G. Smith
63 P. Fleming and Miss W. E. White
64 **J. B. Fitzgerald and Mrs. P. D. Smylie** ②

SECOND ROUND

- **E. Sanchez and Miss M. Navratilova** ① 6-4, 6-4
- P. Aldrich and Miss L. Gregory 6-4, 6-4
- B. Dyke and Miss J. C. Kaplan 7-6, 6-3
- S. Kruger and Miss M. Van Nostrand 7-6, 6-2
- **M. Mortensen and Miss T. Scheuer-Larsen** ⑬ 6-1, 5-7, 6-3
- K. Evernden and Miss J. A. Richardson 6-4, 6-4
- D. MacPherson and Miss J. M. Byrne 6-3, 6-4
- K. Jones and Mrs. S. W. Magers 6-3, 7-6
- **J. Pugh and Miss J. Novotna** ③ 6-3, 6-1
- E. Korita and Miss P. Barg 6-4, 3-6, 6-3
- P. Carter and Miss C. Bakkum 6-4, 6-4
- **R. Leach and Miss P. A. Fendick** ⑩ 7-6, 7-5
- **M. Freeman and Miss L. M. McNeil** ⑯ 6-0, 6-0
- C. Beckman and Miss C. Benjamin 6-4, 7-6
- M. Woodforde and Miss M. Jaggard 6-3, 6-4
- N. A. Fulwood and Miss J. A. Salmon 6-4, 6-4
- **M. J. Bates and Miss J. M. Durie** ⑦ 7-6, 4-6, 6-3
- E. Edwards and Miss E. Reinach 7-6, 7-5
- R. Acuna and Miss J. M. Hetherington 6-4, 3-6, 10-8
- **S. E. Stewart and Miss Z. L. Garrison** ⑭ 6-4, 7-5
- **D. Cahill and Miss N. Provis** ⑪ 6-4, 6-3
- M. Tideman and Miss L. Field 6-3, 6-4
- D. Marcelino and Miss G. Miro 7-6, 6-4
- **P. Annacone and Miss B. Nagelsen** ④ 7-6, 7-6
- **D. T. Visser and Miss R. D. Fairbank** ⑥ 6-4, 6-3
- S. M. Shaw and Miss C. Lindqvist 7-5, 6-3
- T. Pawsat and Miss E. A. Herr 7-5, 3-6, 7-5
- **P. Slozil and Miss S. Graf** ⑨ 6-3, 6-3
- S. Youl and Miss A. L. Minter 6-4, 6-4
- C. A. Bailey and Miss T. A. Catlin 4-6, 6-1, 6-4
- S. Barr and Miss S. L. Collins 6-4, 6-3
- **J. B. Fitzgerald and Mrs. P. D. Smylie** ② 6-1, 6-7, 6-2

THIRD ROUND

- **E. Sanchez and Miss M. Navratilova** ① 6-3, 6-4
- S. Kruger and Miss M. Van Nostrand 7-6 (8-6), 1-6, 6-4
- **M. Mortensen and Miss T. Scheuer-Larsen** ⑬ 4-6, 6-3, 6-2
- K. Jones and Mrs. S. W. Magers 4-6, 7-5, 6-2
- E. Korita and Miss P. Barg 7-6, 2-6, 6-3
- **R. Leach and Miss P. A. Fendick** ⑩ 6-1, 7-6
- **M. Freeman and Miss L. M. McNeil** ⑯ 6-2, 6-7 (3-7), 6-4
- M. Woodforde and Miss M. Jaggard 7-5, 1-6, 6-1
- E. Edwards and Miss E. Reinach
- **S. E. Stewart and Miss Z. L. Garrison** ⑭ 6-2, 3-6, 6-3
- **D. Cahill and Miss N. Provis** ⑪ 6-3, 5-7, 6-0
- **P. Annacone and Miss B. Nagelsen** ④ w/o
- **D. T. Visser and Miss R. D. Fairbank** ⑥ 6-3, 6-2
- T. Pawsat and Miss E. A. Herr w/o
- S. Youl and Miss A. L. Minter 6-2, 6-4
- **J. B. Fitzgerald and Mrs. P. D. Smylie** ② 3-6, 7-5, 6-3

QUARTER-FINALS

- **E. Sanchez and Miss M. Navratilova** ① 6-4, 3-6, 6-3
- K. Jones and Mrs. S. W. Magers w/o
- **R. Leach and Miss P. A. Fendick** ⑩ 7-6 (7-2), 6-4
- **M. Freeman and Miss L. M. McNeil** ⑯ 7-6 (7-4), 6-1
- **S. E. Stewart and Miss Z. L. Garrison** ⑭ 6-1, 7-5
- **D. Cahill and Miss N. Provis** ⑪ w/o
- T. Pawsat and Miss E. A. Herr 7-5, 6-2
- **J. B. Fitzgerald and Mrs. P. D. Smylie** ② w/o

SEMI-FINALS

- K. Jones and Mrs. S. W. Magers 7-6 (8-6), 4-4, ret'd
- **R. Leach and Miss P. A. Fendick** ⑩ 6-4, 5-7, 6-4
- **S. E. Stewart and Miss Z. L. Garrison** ⑭ 7-6 (10-8), 7-5
- **J. B. Fitzgerald and Mrs. P. D. Smylie** ② 6-2, 6-3

FINAL

- K. Jones and Mrs. S. W. Magers 7-6 (7-1), 5-7, 6-4
- **S. E. Stewart and Miss Z. L. Garrison** ⑭ 6-4, 6-7 (10-12), 6-3

Winner
S. E. Stewart and Miss Z. L. Garrison ⑭ 6-1, 7-6 (7-3)

Heavy type denotes seeded players. The encircled figure against names denotes the order in which they have been seeded. (W) = Wild cards. (Q) = Qualifiers. (L) = Lucky losers. The Matches will be the best of three sets. Maiden Names of Competitors will be found on page 44.

Holder: Miss S. L. GOMER

Players who are beaten in the first or second round of the Ladies' Singles Championship and also players only taking part in the Doubles events are entitled to enter for this Event. The Winner will become the holder, for the year only, of a Silver Cup "The All England Ladies' Plate", presented to The All England Lawn Tennis and Croquet Club by the late Mr. A. H. RISELEY, O.B.E. The Winner will receive a silver miniature of the Trophy. Details of Prize Money will be found on page 17.

FIRST ROUND	SECOND ROUND	THIRD ROUND	QUARTER-FINALS	SEMI-FINALS	FINAL
1 **Miss P. A. Fendick** ① ... (U.S.A.)					
2 Bye	Miss P. A. Fendick ① ...				
3 Miss S. L. Collins ... (U.S.A.)		Miss P. A. Fendick ①			
4 Miss P. Barg ... (U.S.A.)	Miss S. L. Collins 6–4, 6–4	6–4, 1–6, 6–4			
5 Miss Y. Koizumi ... (J.)		Miss Y. Koizumi	Miss Y. Koizumi		
6 Miss W. Wood ... (U.S.A.)	Miss Y. Koizumi 6–0, 6–4	6–1, 6–3	1–6, 6–3 ret'd		
7 Miss S. J. Loosemore ... (G.B.)	Miss S. J. Loosemore ...				
8 Bye				Mrs. S. W. Magers ⑧ 6–3, 6–3	
9 **Miss J. M. Hetherington** ⑪ ... (C.)					
10 Bye	Miss J. M. Hetherington ⑪ ...				
11 Miss L. Lapi ... (IT.)		Miss L. Lapi			
12 Miss M. A. Javer ... (G.B.)	Miss L. Lapi 0–6, 6–3, 6–4	6–2, 5–7, 7–5	Mrs. S. W. Magers ⑧		
13 Miss V. Lake ... (G.B.)		**Mrs. S. W. Magers** ⑧	6–2, 6–3		
14 Miss K. A. Steinmetz ... (U.S.A.)	Miss V. Lake 4–6, 7–5, 10–8	6–2, 6–3			
15 Bye					Mrs. S. W. Magers ⑧ 6–1, 6–2
16 **Mrs. S. W. Magers** ⑧ ... (U.S.A.)	Mrs. S. W. Magers ⑧ ...				
17 Miss J. C. Kaplan ... (U.S.A.)					
18 Bye	Miss J. C. Kaplan ...				
19 Miss L. Antonoplis ... (U.S.A.)		Miss J. C. Kaplan			
20 Miss A. Frazier ... (U.S.A.)	Miss A. Frazier 6–3, 6–4	6–0, 3–6, 6–2	Mrs. P. D. Smylie ⑨		
21 Bye		**Mrs. P. D. Smylie** ⑨	6–0, 6–0		
22 Miss A. M. Fernandez ... (U.S.A.)	Miss A. M. Fernandez ...	6–2, 6–3			
23 Bye				Mrs. P. D. Smylie ⑨ 6–4, 7–6 (8–6)	
24 **Mrs. P. D. Smylie** ⑨ ... (A.)	Mrs. P. D. Smylie ⑨ ...				
25 Miss R. McQuillan ... (A.)					
26 Miss L. Field ... (A.)	Miss L. Field 6–7, 6–4, 6–3	Miss L. Field			
27 Miss P. S. Medrado ... (BR.)		6–4, 6–4			
28 Miss C. B. MacGregor ... (U.S.A.)	Miss C. B. MacGregor 6–0, 3–6, 6–2		Miss L. Field		
29 Miss P. Hy ... (H.K.)		Miss J. A. Richardson	6–1, ret'd		
30 Miss J. A. Richardson ... (N.Z.)	Miss J. A. Richardson 7–6, 6–2	6–4, 6–3			
31 Bye					
32 **Mrs. T. A. Harper** ⑥ ... (U.S.A.)	Mrs. T. A. Harper ⑥ ...				
33 **Miss E. S. Pfaff** ⑦ ... (W.G.)	Miss E. S. Pfaff ⑦ ...				
34 Bye					
35 Miss C. Suire ... (F.)		Miss E. S. Pfaff ⑦			
36 Miss T. A. Catlin ... (G.B.)	Miss C. Suire 7–6, 6–3	6–3, 3–6, 11–9	Miss E. S. Pfaff ⑦		
37 Bye			6–3, 7–6 (7–4)		
38 Miss H. A. Ludloff ... (U.S.A.)	Miss H. A. Ludloff ...	Miss H. A. Ludloff			
39 Miss A. Scott ... (A.)		4–6, 6–3, 6–2			
40 Miss L. O'Neill ... (A.)	Miss A. Scott 3–6, 7–5, 4–4, ret'd			Miss S. L. Gomer ⑩ 6–1, 6–2	
41 **Miss S. L. Gomer** ⑩ ... (G.B.)					
42 Bye	Miss S. L. Gomer ⑩ ...				
43 Miss L. Gregory ... (A.)		Miss S. L. Gomer ⑩			
44 Miss C. J. Wood ... (G.B.)	Miss L. Gregory 6–2, 6–2	6–4, 6–4	Miss S. L. Gomer ⑩		
45 Miss A. C. Villagran ... (ARG.)		**Miss B. Schultz** ③	6–3, 7–6 (7–1)		
46 Miss L. C. Gould ... (U.S.A.)	Miss A. C. Villagran 6–1, 4–6, 6–2	6–2, 6–7, 6–1			
47 Bye					Miss S. L. Gomer ⑩ 6–1, 4–6, 6–3
48 **Miss B. Schultz** ③ ... (NTH.)	Miss B. Schultz ③ ...				
49 **Miss R. Zrubakova** ⑤ ... (CZ.)	Miss R. Zrubakova ⑤ ...				
50 Bye					
51 Miss J. M. Byrne ... (A.)		Miss R. Zrubakova ⑤			
52 Bye	Miss J. M. Byrne ...	6–4, 6–2	Miss R. Zrubakova ⑤		
53 Miss M. Lindstrom ... (SW.)		Miss M. Lindstrom	6–0, 1–6, 6–1		
54 Miss A. Simpkin ... (G.B.)	Miss M. Lindstrom 6–3, 6–4	6–2, 7–5			
55 Bye				Miss R. Zrubakova ⑤ 7–5, 7–6 (9–7)	
56 **Miss E. M. Burgin** ⑫ ... (U.S.A.)	Miss E. M. Burgin ⑫ ...				
57 Miss A. L. Grunfeld ... (G.B.)					
58 Miss L. Spadea ... (U.S.A.)	Miss L. Spadea 6–1, 4–6, 6–4	Miss C. MacGregor			
59 Miss C. MacGregor ... (U.S.A.)		6–2, 3–6, 6–4			
60 Miss K. F. Hunter ... (G.B.)	Miss C. MacGregor 6–4, 7–6		Miss C. MacGregor		
61 Miss B. Nagelsen ... (U.S.A.)		**Mrs. C. M. Balestrat** ②	1–6, 6–4, 6–3		
62 Miss M. Jaggard ... (A.)	Miss B. Nagelsen 7–6, 6–1	6–3, 6–4			
63 Bye					
64 **Mrs. C. M. Balestrat** ② ... (A.)	Mrs. C. M. Balestrat ② ...				

Winner: Mrs. S. W. Magers ⑧ 6–1, ret'd

Heavy type denotes seeded players. The encircled figure against names denotes the order in which they have been seeded. The Matches will be the best of three sets.
Maiden Names of Competitors will be found on page 44. For particulars of Abbreviations, see page 43.

EVENT VII.—THE 35 AND OVER GENTLEMEN'S INVITATION SINGLES — Holder: T. R. GULLIKSON

The Winner will become the holder, for the year only, of a Cup presented by The All England Lawn Tennis and Croquet Club. The Winner will receive a miniature Silver Salver, the Runner-up will be presented with a Silver Medal. Details of Prize Money will be found on page 17.

FIRST ROUND	QUARTER-FINALS	SEMI-FINALS	FINAL
1 **T. R. Gullikson** ① (U.S.A.)	**T. R. Gullikson** ① 6–3, 6–3	**T. R. Gullikson** ① 7–5, 6–3	
2 M. Cox (G.B.)			
3 T. S. Okker (NTH.)	A. A. Mayer 6–2, 6–2		**T. R. Gullikson** ① 6–3, 6–4
4 A. A. Mayer (U.S.A.)			
5 **A. D. Roche** ④ (A.)	**A. D. Roche** ④ 6–2, 6–3	**A. D. Roche** ④ 7–5, 6–4	
6 J. Kodes (CZ.)			
7 J. D. Newcombe (A.)	R. L. Stockton 6–4, 7–6 (7–1)		
8 R. L. Stockton (U.S.A.)			**T. R. Gullikson** ① 6–2, 7–6 (13–11)
9 I. Nastase (RU.)	R. Tanner 6–4, 6–7 (3–7), 6–4	**T. E. Gullikson** ③ 6–4, 6–3	
10 R. Tanner (U.S.A.)			
11 J. Fillol (CH.)	**T. E. Gullikson** ③ 7–6 (7–5), 6–3		**T. E. Gullikson** ③ 6–1, 3–6, 6–1
12 **T. E. Gullikson** ③ (U.S.A.)			
13 R. Taylor (G.B.)	M. C. Riessen 4–6, 6–3, 6–4	**R. C. Lutz** ② 4–6, 7–6 (7–4), 6–2	
14 M. C. Riessen (U.S.A.)			
15 J. G. Alexander (A.)	**R. C. Lutz** ② 7–6 (8–6), 6–2		
16 **R. C. Lutz** ② (U.S.A.)			

Heavy type denotes seeded players. The encircled figure against names denotes the order in which they have been seeded. (W) = Wild cards. The Matches will be the best of three sets.
The tie-break will operate at six games all in all three sets. For particulars of Abbreviations, see page 43.

Event VIII.—THE 35 AND OVER GENTLEMEN'S INVITATION DOUBLES — Holders: T. E. GULLIKSON and T. R. GULLIKSON

The Winners will become the holders, for the year only, of a Cup presented by The All England Lawn Tennis and Croquet Club. The Winners will receive miniature Silver Salvers, a Silver Medal will be presented to each of the Runners-up. Details of Prize Money will be found on page 17.

FIRST ROUND	SEMI-FINALS	FINAL
1 **T. E. Gullikson and T. R. Gullikson** ①	R. A. J. Hewitt and F. D. McMillan 6–7 (6–8), 6–3, 6–4	R. A. J. Hewitt and F. D. McMillan 6–2, 7–6 (7–1)
2 R. A. J. Hewitt and F. D. McMillan		
3 **R. L. Case and G. Masters** ④	**R. L. Case and G. Masters** ④ 7–6 (7–5), 4–6, 8–6	
4 R. L. Stockton and R. Tanner		
5 A. Gimeno and R. D. Ralston	**J. D. Newcombe and A. D. Roche** ③ 6–7 (6–8), 6–3, 6–4	K. R. Rosewall and F. S. Stolle 7–6 (7–3), 6–7 (1–7), 10–8
6 **J. D. Newcombe and A. D. Roche** ③		
7 K. R. Rosewall and F. S. Stolle	K. R. Rosewall and F. S. Stolle 7–5, 7–5	R. A. J. Hewitt and F. D. McMillan 6–4, 7–5
8 **M. C. Riessen and S. E. Stewart** ②		

Heavy type denotes seeded players. The encircled figure against names denotes the order in which they have been seeded. (W) = Wild cards. The Matches will be the best of three sets.
The tie-break will operate at six games all in the first two sets only.

151

EVENT IX.—THE BOYS' SINGLES CHAMPIONSHIP

Holder: D. NARGISO

The Winner will become the holder, for the year only, of a Cup presented by The All England Lawn Tennis and Croquet Club. The Winner and Runner-up will each receive a personal prize.

	FIRST ROUND	SECOND ROUND	THIRD ROUND	QUARTER-FINALS	SEMI-FINALS	FINAL
1	J. Stoltenberg ① .... (A.)	J. Stoltenberg ① 6–4, 6–4	J. Stoltenberg ① 6–4, 6–1	J. Stoltenberg ① 6–1, 6–1	N. Pereira ⑥ 4–6, 7–6 (8–6), 6–3	N. Pereira ⑥ 7–6 (7–4), 6–2
2	M. Stringari .... (ARG.)					
3	R. Gana .... (CH.)	G. Carbonari 4–6, 6–4, 6–3				
4	G. Carbonari .... (ARG.)		P. Arnold ⑫ 6–1, 4–6, 6–3			
5	S. Sarli .... (BR.)	S. Sarli 5–7, 6–1, 6–4				
6	C. Delzenne .... (B.)					
7	F. Ofori .... (GH.)	P. Arnold ⑫ 6–2, 6–4				
8	P. Arnold ⑫ .... (ARG.)			N. Pereira ⑥ 7–6 (7–2), 6–4		
9	P. Norval ⑨ .... (S.A.)	P. Norval ⑨ 6–1, 6–3	P. Norval ⑨ 6–3, 6–2			
10	A. Alarcon .... (EC.)					
11	A. Macaraeg .... (PH.)	C. Beecher 6–4, 6–0				
12	C. Beecher .... (G.B.)		N. Pereira ⑥ 5–7, 6–3, 6–4			
13	N. Srichapan .... (THAI.)	M. R. J. Petchey 6–4, 6–1				
14	M. R. J. Petchey .... (G.B.)					
15	D. Nainkin .... (S.A.)	N. Pereira ⑥ 6–3, 6–4				
16	N. Pereira ⑥ .... (V.)					
17	T. Woodbridge ④ .... (A.)	T. Woodbridge ④ 6–0, 6–0	A. Thoms 6–1, 6–7, 6–4	A. Thoms 7–5, 6–4	R. Fromberg ⑦ 6–2, 4–6, 6–3	
18	C-H. Park .... (KOR.)					
19	A. Thoms .... (W.G.)	A. Thoms 6–2, 6–4				
20	J. Palmer .... (U.S.A.)		G. Carneade 6–2, 6–2			
21	G. Carneade .... (EC.)	G. Carneade 6–1, 3–6, 6–3				
22	U. J. Nganga .... (G.B.)					
23	D. Rikl .... (CZ.)	N. Kulti ⑮ 6–4, 6–1				
24	N. Kulti ⑮ .... (SW.)			R. Fromberg ⑦ 3–6, 7–5, 6–1		
25	D. Adams .... (S.A.)	D. Adams 6–4, 6–4	J. Marinov 7–5, 6–2			
26	U. Rahim .... (PAK.)					
27	C. Brandi .... (IT.)	J. Marinov 6–3, 7–5				
28	J. Marinov .... (A.)		R. Fromberg ⑦ 6–2, 7–6			
29	M. Rosset .... (SWZ.)	M. Rosset 6–2, 7–6				
30	A. Ismail .... (IN.)					
31	V. Petrushenko .... (U.S.S.R.)	R. Fromberg ⑦ 4–6, 7–5, 6–3				
32	R. Fromberg ⑦ .... (A.)					
33	G. Ivanisevic ⑤ ...... (YU.)	G. Ivanisevic ⑤ 3–6, 6–3, 6–2	G. Ivanisevic ⑤ 6–3, 6–2	G. Ivanisevic ⑤ 7–6 (7–4), 7–6 (7–3)	A. Cherkasov ③ 7–5, 6–1, 6–4	
34	M. Blackman .... (G.B.)					
35	D. Bishop .... (G.B.)	G. Koves 6–3, 6–0				
36	G. Koves .... (HU.)		J. Stark 6–1, 6–4			
37	T. Zdrazila .... (CZ.)	J. Stark 7–5, 6–2				
38	J. Stark .... (U.S.A.)					
39	Y. Yamamoto .... (J.)	J. Lenton 6–3, 3–6, 6–3				
40	L. E. Lenton .... (M.)			A. Cherkasov ③ 7–5, 7–5		
41	L. E. Herrera ⑭ ...... (M.)	L. E. Herrera ⑭ 6–3, 6–2	L. E. Herrera ⑭ 6–3, 6–2			
42	T-H. Kong .... (KOR.)					
43	C. Caratti .... (IT.)	C. Caratti 6–0, 6–2				
44	R. Rajpal .... (IN.)		A. Cherkasov ③ 6–1, 6–3			
45	C. Wilkinson .... (G.B.)	D. Di Lucia 6–3, 3–6, 6–3				
46	D. Di Lucia .... (U.S.A.)					
47	M. Larsson .... (SW.)	A. Cherkasov ③ 6–3, 6–7, 6–3				
48	A. Cherkasov ③ .... (U.S.S.R.)					
49	Z. Ali ⑧ .... (IN.)	Z. Ali ⑧ 6–7, 6–3, 6–2	L. Jonsson 6–3, 6–4	L. Jonsson 6–4, 4–6, 6–3	G. Raoux ⑬ 5–7, 6–1, 6–4	
50	A. Florent .... (A.)					
51	L. Jonsson .... (SW.)	L. Jonsson 6–1, 6–3				
52	A. Batie .... (N.Z.)		H-C. Shin 6–4, 6–2			
53	H-C. Shin .... (KOR.)	H-C. Shin 6–4, 4–6, 6–3				
54	R. Teofilo .... (BR.)					
55	J. J. Hunter .... (G.B.)	R. Jabali ⑩ 3–6, 6–3, 8–6				
56	R. Jabali ⑩ .... (BR.)			G. Raoux ⑬ 7–6 (7–5), 6–3		
57	G. Raoux ⑬ .... (F.)	G. Raoux ⑬ 6–3, 7–5	G. Raoux ⑬ 6–0, 6–3			
58	G. Lopez .... (SP.)					
59	B. Wijaya .... (IND.)	B. Wijaya 7–6, 6–3				
60	J-H. Shin .... (KOR.)		M. Hadad 4–6, 6–1, 10–8			
61	M. Hadad .... (COL.)	M. Hadad 6–2, 6–4				
62	E. Fourie .... (S.A.)					
63	L. Sidor .... (POL.)	L. Sidor 6–3, 4–6, 2–3, ret'd				
64	J. Anderson ② .... (A.)					

Heavy type denotes seeded players. The encircled figure against names denotes the order in which they have been seeded. The Committee reserves the right to alter the seeding order in the event of withdrawals. The Matches will be the best of three sets. For particulars of Abbreviations, see page 43.

EVENT X.—THE BOYS' DOUBLES CHAMPIONSHIP

Holders: J. STOLTENBERG and T. WOODBRIDGE

The Winners and Runners-up will each receive a personal prize.

	FIRST ROUND	SECOND ROUND	QUARTER-FINALS	SEMI-FINALS	FINAL
1	J. Stoltenberg and T. Woodbridge ①	J. Stoltenberg and T. Woodbridge ① 6–0, 6–2	J. Stoltenberg and T. Woodbridge ① 6–2, 7–6 (7–1)	J. Stoltenberg and T. Woodbridge ① 6–3, 6–2	J. Stoltenberg and T. Woodbridge ① 6–3, 6–7 (6–8), 7–5
2	U. Rahim and Y. Yamamoto				
3	M. Rosset and A. Thoms	L. Jonsson and G. Raoux 7–6, 7–6			
4	L. Jonsson and G. Raoux				
5	A. Ismail and N. Srichapan	A. Alarcon and R. Jabali 6–7, 6–1, 6–4	A. Alarcon and R. Jabali 6–4, 5–7, 8–6		
6	A. Alarcon and R. Jabali				
7	A. Florent and J. Marinov	A. Florent and J. Marinov 3–6, 6–4, 8–6			
8	M. Blackman and J. Palmer ⑦				
9	C. Brandi and C. Caratti ④	C. Brandi and C. Caratti ④ 6–3, 6–2	C. Brandi and C. Caratti ④ 6–2, 7–5	C. Brandi and C. Caratti ④ 2–3, ret'd	
10	R. Gana and F. Rivera				
11	C. Johnson and G. Lopez	J. J. Hunter and C. Wilkinson 6–3, 6–4			
12	J. J. Hunter and C. Wilkinson				
13	D. Nainkin and P. Norval	D. Nainkin and P. Norval 6–3, 6–2	C. Beecher and M. R. J. Petchey 7–6 (7–3), 0–6, 6–4		
14	G. Koves and L. Sidor				
15	S. Leblanc and G. Rusedski	C. Beecher and M. R. J. Petchey ⑥ 6–4, 6–2			
16	C. Beecher and M. R. J. Petchey ⑥				
17	D. Rikl and T. Zdrazila ⑤	D. Rikl and T. Zdrazila ⑤ 6–4, 6–2	D. Rikl and T. Zdrazila ⑤ 6–4, 6–4	D. Rikl and T. Zdrazila ⑤ 6–3, 2–6, 6–4	D. Rikl and T. Zdrazila ⑤ 6–4, 6–3
18	C-H. Park and H-C. Shin				
19	G. Carneade and M. Stringari	A. Batie and R. Rajpal 7–6, 6–2			
20	A. Batie and R. Rajpal				
21	J. Macaraeg and B. Wijaya	D. Gold and D. Ireland 6–3, 6–4	A. Cherkasov and V. Petrushenko 6–2, 6–3		
22	D. Gold and D. Ireland				
23	J. Lenton and U. J. Nganga	A. Cherkasov and V. Petrushenko ③ 7–6, 7–5			
24	A. Cherkasov and V. Petrushenko ③				
25	J. Anderson and R. Fromberg ⑧	R. Teofilo and S. Sarli " w.o	D. Di Lucia and J. Stark 6–3, 6–2	D. Di Lucia and J. Stark 7–5, 4–6, 6–2	
26	R. Teofilo and S. Sarli				
27	D. Di Lucia and J. Stark	D. Di Lucia and J. Stark 6–3, 3–6, 6–3			
28	M. Hadad and L. E. Herrera				
29	D. Adams and E. Fourie	D. Adams and E. Fourie 6–3, 6–2	N. Kulti and M. Larsson 6–4, 5–7, 13–11		
30	T-H. Kong and J-H. Shin				
31	N. Kulti and M. Larsson	N. Kulti and M. Larsson 7–6, 2–6, 7–7, ret'd			
32	Z. Ali and G. Ivanisevic ②				

Winner: **J. Stoltenberg and T. Woodbridge ① 6–4, 1–6, 7–5**

Heavy type denotes seeded players. The encircled figure against names denotes the order in which they have been seeded. The Committee reserves the right to alter the seeding order in the event of withdrawals. The Matches will be the best of three sets.

EVENT XI.—THE GIRLS' SINGLES CHAMPIONSHIP

Holder: Miss N. ZVEREVA

The Winner will become the holder, for the year only, of a Cup presented by The All England Lawn Tennis and Croquet Club. The Winner and Runner-up will each receive a personal prize.

FIRST ROUND	SECOND ROUND	THIRD ROUND	QUARTER-FINALS	SEMI-FINALS	FINAL

```
 1  Miss B. Schultz ①          (NTH.)   Miss B. Schultz ①        6–0, 6–2
 2  Miss J. Moreno             (ARG.)                                         Miss B. Schultz ①
 3  Miss S. Czopek             (POL.)   Miss Y. Segal            6–2, 7–5                  6–1, 6–3
 4  Miss Y. Segal              (ISR.)                                                              Miss B. Schultz ①
 5  Miss C. Tessi              (ARG.)   Miss A. Grossman        6–3, 7–6      Miss A. Grossman      6–7 (5–7), 7–5, 8–6
 6  Miss A. Grossman           (U.S.A.)                                       3–6, 6–4, 6–2
 7  Miss A. S. Hill            (G.B.)   Miss S. Appelmans ⑪      6–3, 6–3
 8  Miss S. Appelmans ⑪        (G.B.)                                                                        Miss B. Schultz ①
 9  Miss S. J. Loosemore ⑭     (G.B.)   Miss S. J. Loosemore ⑭   6–0, 6–2                                    6–2, 6–2
10  Miss A. Casas              (SP.)                                          Miss K. Date
11  Miss K. Date               (J.)     Miss K. Date            6–0, 6–2                  6–2, 6–4
12  Miss O. Thampensri         (THAI.)                                                             Miss M. Laval
13  Miss O. Bouchabou          (ALG.)   Miss O. Bouchabou       0–6, 6–2, 6–4  Miss M. Laval         6–1, 6–4
14  Miss C. Brause             (U.)                                          7–5, 6–1
15  Miss M. Laval              (F.)     Miss M. Laval           7–5, 6–3
16  Miss L. Lapi ⑥             (IT.)
17  Miss A. Dechaume ④         (F.)     Miss A. Dechaume ④       6–1, 6–0
18  Miss A. Chorlton           (G.B.)                                        Miss A. Dechaume ④
19  Miss V. Humphreys-Davies   (G.B.)   Miss A. Farley          6–1, 6–4                  6–4, 6–4
20  Miss A. Farley             (U.S.A.)                                                            Miss A. Dechaume ④
21  Miss C. P. Toleafoa        (N.Z.)   Miss C. P. Toleafoa     2–6, 6–3, 10–8  Miss C. P. Toleafoa   6–1, 6–0
22  Miss N. Dahlman            (FI.)                                          6–4, 7–5
23  Miss A. Kaul               (BR.)    Miss A. Kaul            7–5, 6–2
24  Miss V. Martinek ⑩         (W.G.)                                                                       Miss A. Frazier ⑤
25  Miss C. Caverzasio ⑨       (IT.)    Miss C. Caverzasio ⑨     6–2, 6–7, 6–2                               7–5, 7–6 (7–2)
26  Miss P. Collantes          (PE.)                                         Miss A. Coetzer
27  Miss B-S. Choi             (KOR.)   Miss A. Coetzer         7–5, 6–3                  7–5, 6–4
28  Miss A. Coetzer            (S.A.)                                                             Miss A. Frazier ⑤
29  Miss M. McGrath            (U.S.A.) Miss M. McGrath         6–3, 6–1      Miss A. Frazier ⑤     0–6, 6–2, 6–3
30  Miss S. L. Smith           (G.B.)                                        3–6, 6–2, 11–9
31  Miss A. M. Niepel          (G.B.)   Miss A. Frazier ⑤       7–5, 6–4
32  Miss A. Frazier ⑤          (U.S.A.)
33  Miss J. Pospisilova ⑧      (CZ.)    Miss J. Pospisilova ⑧    6–0, 6–3
34  Miss M. Zivec              (W.G.)                                        Miss J. Pospisilova ⑧
35  Miss M. Mroz               (POL.)   Miss M. Mroz            7–5, 6–3                  6–2, 6–2
36  Miss G. Villiger           (SWZ.)                                                            Miss J. Pospisilova ⑧
37  Miss K. R. Radford         (A.)     Miss K. R. Radford      6–2, 6–1       Miss R. McQuillan ⑬   6–7 (3–7), 7–6 (7–3), 6–1
38  Miss D. Fortuna            (IND.)                                         2–6, 7–6, 8–6
39  Miss N. C. Topper          (G.B.)   Miss R. McQuillan ⑬      6–1, 6–4
40  Miss R. McQuillan ⑬        (A.)                                                                        Miss J. Pospisilova ⑧
41  Miss J.-A. Faull ⑫         (A.)     Miss J.-A. Faull ⑫       6–2, 7–5                                    6–4, 6–3
42  Miss M. R. Bowrey          (A.)                                          Miss J.-A. Faull ⑫
43  Miss F. Li                 (CHI.)   Miss E. Nieto           7–6, 6–2                  6–2, 6–1
44  Miss E. Nieto              (V.)                                                               Miss J. Halard ③
45  Miss L. J. Nimmo           (G.B.)   Miss M. Ekstrand        7–6, 6–0       Miss J. Halard ③      6–1, 6–4
46  Miss M. Ekstrand           (SW.)                                         7–6, 6–4
47  Miss R. Gaddie             (S.A.)   Miss J. Halard ③        6–4, 7–6
48  Miss J. Halard ③           (F.)
49  Miss E. Derly ⑦            (F.)     Miss E. Derly ⑦         7–5, 6–4
50  Miss L. Spadea             (U.S.A.)                                      Miss E. Derly ⑦
51  Miss R. Hiraki             (J.)     Miss R. Hiraki          6–3, 6–2                  3–6, 6–2, 6–4
52  Miss N. Biletskaia         (U.S.S.R.)                                                          Miss E. Derly ⑦
53  Miss L. Randmaa            (C.)     Miss M. Drake           6–2, 6–1       Miss M. Drake         4–6, 6–2, 7–5
54  Miss M. Drake              (C.)                                          7–5, 6–3
55  Miss J. Muir               (ZIM.)   Miss S. Frankl ⑮        6–1, 6–1
56  Miss S. Frankl ⑮           (W.G.)                                                                       Miss E. Derly ⑦
57  Miss N. Medvedeva ⑯        (U.S.S.R.) Miss N. Medvedeva ⑯   6–2, 6–2                                    6–1, 6–4
58  Miss S. Italiano           (C.)                                         Miss N. Medvedeva ⑯
59  Miss M. F. Labat           (ARG.)   Miss D. Graham          6–2, 7–6                  6–2, 6–3
60  Miss D. Graham             (U.S.A.)                                                            Miss N. Medvedeva ⑯
61  Miss S. Okada              (J.)     Miss S-T. Wang          1–6, 7–6, 6–2  Miss N. Sawamatsu     6–3, 6–2
62  Miss S-T. Wang             (TAI.)                                        6–2, 6–4
63  Miss N. Sawamatsu          (J.)     Miss N. Sawamatsu       6–2, 6–4
64  Miss R. Zrubakova ②        (CZ.)
```

Miss B. Schultz ① 6–7 (5–7), 6–4, 6–2

Miss E. Derly ⑦ 6–3, 6–3

Miss B. Schultz ① 7–6 (7–5), 6–1

Heavy type denotes seeded players. The encircled figure against names denotes the order in which they have been seeded. The Committee reserves the right to alter the seeding order in the event of withdrawals. The Matches will be the best of three sets. For particulars of Abbreviations, see page 43.

EVENT XII.—THE GIRLS' DOUBLES CHAMPIONSHIP

Holders: Miss N. MEDVEDEVA and Miss N. ZVEREVA

The Winners and Runners-up will each receive a personal prize.

FIRST ROUND	SECOND ROUND	QUARTER-FINALS	SEMI-FINALS	FINAL

```
 1  Miss A. Dechaume and Miss E. Derly ①      Miss A. Dechaume and Miss E. Derly ①
 2  Bye                                                                          Miss A. Dechaume and Miss E. Derly ①
 3  Miss K. Date and Miss S. Okada            Miss N. Dahlman and Miss C. Tessi 6–7, 6–0, 6–2   6–3, 4–6, 6–3
 4  Miss N. Dahlman and Miss C. Tessi
 5  Miss S. Italiano and Miss L. Randmaa      Miss S. Italiano and Miss L. Randmaa 7–6, 6–3     Miss M. R. Bowrey and
 6  Miss R. Hiraki and Miss S-T. Wang                                          Miss K. R. Radford
 7  Miss S. Czopek and Miss M. Mroz           Miss M. R. Bowrey and Miss K. R. Radford ⑥        6–0, 6–2
 8  Miss M. R. Bowrey and Miss K. R. Radford ⑥     7–6, 6–2
 9  Miss A. Frazier and Miss L. Spadea ④      Miss A. Frazier and Miss L. Spadea ④
10  Bye                                                                          Miss A. Frazier and
11  Miss A. Casas and Miss G. Villiger        Miss A. S. Hill and Miss Y. Segal 1–6, 6–3, 6–3   Miss L. Spadea ④
12  Miss A. S. Hill and Miss Y. Segal                                          w/o
13  Miss M. F. Labat and Miss C. P. Toleafoa  Miss M. F. Labat and Miss C. P. Toleafoa 6–2, 6–2  Miss N. Biletskaia and
14  Miss O. Bouchabou and Miss J. Muir                                         Miss N. Medvedeva
15  Miss A. Chorlton and Miss M. Drake        Miss N. Biletskaia and Miss N. Medvedeva ⑧        6–3, 6–0
16  Miss N. Biletskaia and Miss N. Medvedeva ⑧    6–2, 6–1
17  Miss A. Grossman and Miss M. McGrath ⑤    Miss A. Grossman and Miss M. McGrath ⑤
18  Miss F. Li and Miss N. Sawamatsu                                           Miss A. Grossman and
19  Miss S. L. Smith and Miss N. C. Topper    Miss S. L. Smith and Miss N. C. Topper 6–4, 6–4   Miss M. McGrath ⑤
20  Miss C. Brause and Miss A. Kaul                                            7–5, 6–2
21  Miss P. Collantes and Miss O. Thampensri  Miss A. Farley and Miss D. Graham 6–3, 6–0        Miss J. Pospisilova and
22  Miss A. Farley and Miss D. Graham                                          Miss R. Zrubakova ③
23  Bye                                       Miss J. Pospisilova and Miss R. Zrubakova ③       7–6 (7–5), 6–2
24  Miss J. Pospisilova and Miss R. Zrubakova ③
25  Miss J. Halard and Miss M. Laval ⑦        Miss J. Halard and Miss M. Laval ⑦   6–2, 6–2     Miss J. Halard and
26  Miss J. Moreno and Miss E. Nieto                                           Miss M. Laval
27  Miss V. Martinek and Miss M. Zivec        Miss V. Humphreys-Davies and Miss S. J. Loosemore  6–1, 6–2
28  Miss V. Humphreys-Davies and Miss S. J. Loosemore    6–7 (4–7), 6–4, 13–11
29  Miss A. Coetzer and Miss R. Gaddie        Miss A. Coetzer and Miss R. Gaddie 6–1, 6–2       Miss J.-A. Faull and
30  Miss B-S. Choi and Miss D. Fortuna                                         Miss R. McQuillan ②
31  Bye                                       Miss J.-A. Faull and Miss R. McQuillan ②          3–6, 7–6 (7–5), 6–3
32  Miss J.-A. Faull and Miss R. McQuillan ②      2–6, 6–2, 7–5
```

Miss A. Dechaume and Miss E. Derly ① 6–3, 6–2

Miss J.-A. Faull and Miss R. McQuillan ② 3–6, 7–6 (7–3), 6–1

Miss J.-A. Faull and Miss R. McQuillan ② 4–6, 6–2, 6–3

Heavy type denotes seeded players. The encircled figure against names denotes the order in which they have been seeded. The Committee reserves the right to alter the seeding order in the event of withdrawals. The Matches will be the best of three sets.

THE CHAMPIONSHIP ROLL
Champions and Runners-up

MEN'S SINGLES

1877—S. W. Gore
W. C. Marshall
1878—P. F. Hadow
S. W. Gore
★1879—J. T. Hartley
V. St. L. Goold
1880—J. T. Hartley
H. F. Lawford
1881—W. Renshaw
J. T. Hartley
1882—W. Renshaw
E. Renshaw
1883—W. Renshaw
E. Renshaw
1884—W. Renshaw
H. F. Lawford
1885—W. Renshaw
H. F. Lawford
1886—W. Renshaw
H. F. Lawford
★1887—H. F. Lawford
E. Renshaw
1888—E. Renshaw
H. F. Lawford
1889—W. Renshaw
E. Renshaw
1890—W. J. Hamilton
W. Renshaw
★1891—W. Baddeley
J. Pim
1892—W. Baddeley
J. Pim
1893—J. Pim
W. Baddeley
1894—J. Pim
W. Baddeley

★1895—W. Baddeley
W. V. Eaves
1896—H. S. Mahony
W. Baddeley
1897—R. F. Doherty
H. S. Mahony
1898—R. F. Doherty
H. L. Doherty
1899—R. F. Doherty
A. W. Gore
1900—R. F. Doherty
S. H. Smith
1901—A. W. Gore
R. F. Doherty
1902—H. L. Doherty
A. W. Gore
1903—H. L. Doherty
F. L. Riseley
1904—H. L. Doherty
F. L. Riseley
1905—H. L. Doherty
N. E. Brookes
1906—H. L. Doherty
F. L. Riseley
★1907—N. E. Brookes
A. W. Gore
★1908—A. W. Gore
H. Roper Barrett
1909—A. W. Gore
M. J. G. Ritchie

1910—A. F. Wilding
A. W. Gore
1911—A. F. Wilding
H. Roper Barrett
1912—A. F. Wilding
A. W. Gore
1913—A. F. Wilding
M. E. McLoughlin
1914—N. E. Brookes
A. F. Wilding
1919—G. L. Patterson
N. E. Brookes
1920—W. T. Tilden
G. L. Patterson
1921—W. T. Tilden
B. I. C. Norton
★†1922—G. L. Patterson
R. Lycett
1923—W. M. Johnston
F. T. Hunter
1924—J. Borotra
R. Lacoste
1925—R. Lacoste
J. Borotra
1926—J. Borotra
H. Kinsey
1927—H. Cochet
J. Borotra
1928—R. Lacoste
H. Cochet

1929—H. Cochet
J. Borotra
1930—W. T. Tilden
W. Allison
1931—S. B. Wood
F. X. Shields
1932—H. E. Vines
H. W. Austin
1933—H. Crawford
H. E. Vines
1934—F. J. Perry
J. H. Crawford
1935—F. J. Perry
G. von Cramm
1936—F. J. Perry
G. von Cramm
★1937—J. D. Budge
G. von Cramm
1938—J. D. Budge
H. W. Austin
★1939—R. L. Riggs
E. T. Cooke
★1946—Y. Petra
G. E. Brown
1947—J. Kramer
T. Brown
★1948—R. Falkenburg
J. E. Bromwich
1949—F. R. Schroeder
J. Drobny
★1950—B. Patty
F. A. Sedgman
1951—R. Savitt
K. McGregor
1952—F. A. Sedgman
J. Drobny

★1953—V. Seixas
K. Nielsen
1954—J. Drobny
K. R. Rosewall
1955—T. Trabert
K. Nielsen
★1956—L. A. Hoad
K. R. Rosewall
1957—L. A. Hoad
A. J. Cooper
★1958—A. J. Cooper
N. A. Fraser
★1959—A. Olmedo
R. Laver
★1960—N. A. Fraser
R. Laver
1961—R. Laver
C. R. McKinley
1962—R. Laver
M. F. Mulligan
★1963—C. R. McKinley
F. S. Stolle
1964—R. Emerson
F. S. Stolle
1965—R. Emerson
F. S. Stolle
1966—M. Santana
R. D. Ralston
1967—J. D. Newcombe
W. P. Bungert
1968—R. Laver
A. D. Roche
1969—R. Laver
J. D. Newcombe
1970—J. D. Newcombe
K. R. Rosewall

1971—J. D. Newcombe
S. R. Smith
★1972—S. R. Smith
I. Nastase
★1973—J. Kodes
A. Metreveli
1974—J. S. Connors
K. R. Rosewall
1975—A. R. Ashe
J. S. Connors
1976—B. Borg
I. Nastase
1977—B. Borg
J. S. Connors
1978—B. Borg
J. S. Connors
1979—B. Borg
R. Tanner
1980—B. Borg
J. P. McEnroe
1981—J. P. McEnroe
B. Borg
1982—J. S. Connors
J. P. McEnroe
1983—J. P. McEnroe
C. J. Lewis
1984—J. P. McEnroe
J. S. Connors
1985—B. Becker
K. Curren
1986—B. Becker
I. Lendl
1987—P. Cash
I. Lendl

MEN'S DOUBLES

1879—L. R. Erskine and H. F. Lawford
F. Durant and G. E. Tabor
1880—W. Renshaw and E. Renshaw
O. E. Woodhouse and C. J. Cole
1881—W. Renshaw and E. Renshaw
W. J. Down and H. Vaughan
1882—J. T. Hartley and R. T. Richardson
J. G. Horn and C. B. Russell
1883—C. W. Grinstead and C. E. Welldon
C. B. Russell and R. T. Milford
1884—W. Renshaw and E. Renshaw
E. W. Lewis and E. L. Williams
1885—W. Renshaw and E. Renshaw
C. E. Farrar and A. J. Stanley
1886—W. Renshaw and E. Renshaw
C. E. Farrar and A. J. Stanley
1887—P. Bowes-Lyon and H. W. W. Wilberforce
J. H. Crispe and Barratt Smith
1888—W. Renshaw and E. Renshaw
P. Bowes-Lyon and H. W. W. Wilberforce
1889—W. Renshaw and E. Renshaw
E. W. Lewis and G. W. Hillyard
1890—J. Pim and F. O. Stoker
E. W. Lewis and G. W. Hillyard
1891—W. Baddeley and H. Baddeley
J. Pim and F. O. Stoker
1892—H. S. Barlow and E. W. Lewis
W. Baddeley and H. Baddeley
1893—J. Pim and F. O. Stoker
E. W. Lewis and H. S. Barlow
1894—W. Baddeley and H. Baddeley
H. S. Barlow and C. H. Martin
1895—W. Baddeley and H. Baddeley
E. W. Lewis and W. V. Eaves
1896—W. Baddeley and H. Baddeley
R. F. Doherty and H. A. Nisbet
1897—R. F. Doherty and H. L. Doherty
W. Baddeley and H. Baddeley
1898—R. F. Doherty and H. L. Doherty
H. A. Nisbet and C. Hobart
1899—R. F. Doherty and H. L. Doherty
H. A. Nisbet and C. Hobart
1900—R. F. Doherty and H. L. Doherty
H. Roper Barrett and H. A. Nisbet
1901—R. F. Doherty and H. L. Doherty
Dwight Davis and Holcombe Ward
1902—S. H. Smith and F. L. Riseley
R. F. Doherty and H. L. Doherty
1903—R. F. Doherty and H. L. Doherty
S. H. Smith and F. L. Riseley
1904—R. F. Doherty and H. L. Doherty
S. H. Smith and F. L. Riseley
1905—R. F. Doherty and H. L. Doherty
S. H. Smith and F. L. Riseley
1906—S. H. Smith and F. L. Riseley
R. F. Doherty and H. L. Doherty
1907—N. E. Brookes and A. F. Wilding
B. C. Wright and K. C. Behr
1908—A. F. Wilding and M. J. G. Ritchie
A. W. Gore and H. Roper Barrett
1909—A. W. Gore and H. Roper Barrett
S. N. Doust and H. A. Parker
1910—A. F. Wilding and M. J. G. Ritchie
A. W. Gore and H. Roper Barrett
1911—M. Decugis and A. H. Gobert
M. J. G. Ritchie and A. F. Wilding

1912—H. Roper Barrett and C. P. Dixon
M. Decugis and A. H. Gobert
1913—H. Roper Barrett and C. P. Dixon
F. W. Rahe and H. Kleinschroth
1914—N. E. Brookes and A. F. Wilding
H. Roper Barrett and C. P. Dixon
1919—R. V. Thomas and P. O'Hara-Wood
R. Lycett and R. W. Heath
1920—R. N. Williams and C. S. Garland
A. R. F. Kingscote and J. C. Parke
1921—R. Lycett and M. Woosnam
F. G. Lowe and A. H. Lowe
† 1922—R. Lycett and J. O. Anderson
G. L. Patterson and P. O'Hara-Wood
1923—R. Lycett and L. A. Godfree
Count de Gomar and E. Flaquer
1924—F. T. Hunter and V. Richards
R. N. Williams and W. M. Washburn
1925—J. Borotra and R. Lacoste
J. Hennessey and R. Casey
1926—H. Cochet and J. Brugnon
V. Richards and H. Kinsey
1927—F. T. Hunter and W. T. Tilden
J. Brugnon and J. Cochet
1928—H. Cochet and J. Brugnon
G. L. Patterson and J. B. Hawkes
1929—W. Allison and J. Van Ryn
J. C. Gregory and I. G. Collins
1930—W. Allison and J. Van Ryn
J. H. Doeg and G. M. Lott
1931—G. M. Lott and J. Van Ryn
H. Cochet and J. Brugnon
1932—J. Borotra and J. Brugnon
G. P. Hughes and F. J. Perry
1933—J. Borotra and J. Brugnon
R. Nunoi and J. Satoh
1934—G. M. Lott and L. R. Stoefen
J. Borotra and J. Brugnon
1935—J. H. Crawford and A. K. Quist
W. Allison and J. Van Ryn
1936—G. P. Hughes and C. R. D. Tuckey
C. E. Hare and F. H. D. Wilde
1937—J. D. Budge and G. Mako
G. P. Hughes and C. R. D. Tuckey
1938—J. D. Budge and G. Mako
H. Henkel and G. von Metaxa
1939—R. L. Riggs and E. T. Cooke
C. E. Hare and F. H. D. Wilde
1946—T. Brown and J. Kramer
G. E. Brown and D. Pails
1947—R. Falkenburg and J. Kramer
A. J. Mottram and O. W. Sidwell
1948—J. E. Bromwich and F. A. Sedgman
T. Brown and G. Mulloy
1949—R. Gonzales and F. Parker
G. Mulloy and F. R. Schroeder
1950—J. E. Bromwich and A. K. Quist
G. E. Brown and O. W. Sidwell
1951—K. McGregor and F. A. Sedgman
J. Drobny and E. W. Sturgess
1952—K. McGregor and F. A. Sedgman
V. Seixas and E. W. Sturgess
1953—L. A. Hoad and K. R. Rosewall
R. N. Hartwig and M. G. Rose
1954—R. N. Hartwig and M. G. Rose
V. Seixas and T. Trabert

1955—R. N. Hartwig and L. A. Hoad
N. A. Fraser and K. R. Rosewall
1956—L. A. Hoad and K. R. Rosewall
N. Pietrangeli and O. Sirola
1957—G. Mulloy and B. Patty
N. A. Fraser and L. A. Hoad
1958—S. Davidson and U. Schmidt
A. J. Cooper and N. A. Fraser
1959—R. Emerson and N. A. Fraser
R. Laver and R. Mark
1960—R. H. Osuna and R. D. Ralston
M. G. Davies and R. K. Wilson
1961—R. Emerson and N. A. Fraser
R. A. J. Hewitt and F. S. Stolle
1962—R. A. J. Hewitt and F. S. Stolle
B. Jovanovic and N. Pilic
1963—R. H. Osuna and A. Palafox
J. C. Barclay and P. Darmon
1964—R. A. J. Hewitt and F. S. Stolle
R. Emerson and K. N. Fletcher
1965—J. D. Newcombe and A. D. Roche
K. N. Fletcher and R. A. J. Hewitt
1966—K. N. Fletcher and J. D. Newcombe
W. W. Bowrey and O. K. Davidson
1967—R. A. J. Hewitt and F. D. McMillan
R. Emerson and K. N. Fletcher
1968—J. D. Newcombe and A. D. Roche
K. R. Rosewall and F. S. Stolle
1969—J. D. Newcombe and A. D. Roche
T. S. Okker and M. C. Riessen
1970—J. D. Newcombe and A. D. Roche
K. R. Rosewall and F. S. Stolle
1971—R. S. Emerson and R. G. Laver
A. R. Ashe and R. D. Ralston
1972—R. A. J. Hewitt and F. D. McMillan
S. R. Smith and E. J. van Dillen
1973—J. S. Connors and I. Nastase
J. R. Cooper and N. A. Fraser
1974—J. D. Newcombe and A. D. Roche
R. C. Lutz and S. R. Smith
1975—V. Gerulaitis and A. Mayer
C. Dowdeswell and A. J. Stone
1976—B. E. Gottfried and R. Ramirez
R. L. Case and G. Masters
1977—R. L. Case and G. Masters
J. G. Alexander and P. C. Dent
1978—R. A. J. Hewitt and F. D. McMillan
P. Fleming and J. P. McEnroe
1979—P. Fleming and J. P. McEnroe
B. E. Gottfried and R. Ramirez
1980—P. McNamara and P. McNamee
R. C. Lutz and S. R. Smith
1981—P. Fleming and J. P. McEnroe
R. C. Lutz and S. R. Smith
1982—P. McNamara and P. McNamee
P. Fleming and J. P. McEnroe
1983—P. Fleming and J. P. McEnroe
T. E. Gullikson and T. R. Gullikson
1984—P. Fleming and J. P. McEnroe
P. Cash and P. McNamee
1985—H. P. Guenthardt and B. Taroczy
P. Cash and J. B. Fitzgerald
1986—J. Nystrom and M. Wilander
G. Donnelly and P. Fleming
1987—K. Flach and R. Seguso
S. Casal and E. Sanchez

154

THE CHAMPIONSHIP ROLL

LADIES' SINGLES

1884—Miss M. Watson
Miss Watson
1885—Miss M. Watson
Miss B. Bingley
1886—Miss B. Bingley
Miss M. Watson
1887—Miss L. Dod
Miss B. Bingley
1888—Miss L. Dod
Mrs. G. W. Hillyard
★1889—Mrs G. W. Hillyard
Miss L. Rice
★1890—Miss L. Rice
Miss Jacks
★1891—Miss L. Dod
Mrs. G. W. Hillyard
1892—Miss L. Dod
Mrs. G. W. Hillyard
1893—Miss L. Dod
Mrs. G. W. Hillyard
★1894—Mrs. G. W. Hillyard
Miss L. Rice
★1895—Miss C. Cooper
Miss Jackson
1896—Miss C. Cooper
Mrs. Pickering
1897—Mrs. G. W. Hillyard
Miss C. Cooper
★1898—Miss C. Cooper
Miss Martin
1899—Mrs G. W. Hillyard
Miss C. Cooper
1900—Mrs G. W. Hillyard
Miss C. Cooper
1901—Mrs. A. Sterry
Mrs. G. W. Hillyard
1902—Miss M. E. Robb
Mrs. A. Sterry

★1903—Miss D. K. Douglass
Miss E. W. Thomson
1904—Miss D. K. Douglass
Mrs. A. Sterry
1905—Miss M. Sutton
Miss D. K. Douglass
1906—Miss D. K. Douglass
Miss M. Sutton
1907—Miss M. Sutton
Mrs. Lambert Chambers
★1908—Mrs. A. Sterry
Miss A. M. Morton
★1909—Miss D. P. Boothby
Miss A. M. Morton
1910—Mrs. Lambert Chambers
Miss D. P. Boothby
1911—Mrs. Lambert Chambers
Miss D. P. Boothby
★1912—Mrs. D. R. Larcombe
Mrs. A. Sterry
★1913—Mrs. Lambert Chambers
Mrs. R. J. McNair
1914—Mrs. Lambert Chambers
Mrs. D. R. Larcombe
1919—Mlle. S. Lenglen
Mrs. Lambert Chambers
1920—Mlle S. Lenglen
Mrs. Lambert Chambers
1921—Mlle. S. Lenglen
Miss E. Ryan
†1922—Mlle. S. Lenglen
Mrs. Mallory
1923—Mlle. S. Lenglen
Miss K. McKane
1924—Miss K. McKane
Miss H. Wills
1925—Mlle. S. Lenglen
Miss J. Fry

1926—Mrs. L. A. Godfree
Sta. L. de Alvarez
1927—Miss H. Wills
Sta. L. de Alvarez
1928—Miss H. Wills
Sta. L. de Alvarez
1929—Miss H. Wills
Miss H. H. Jacobs
1930—Mrs. F. S. Moody
Miss E. Ryan
★1931—Fraulein C. Aussem
Fraulein H. Krahwinkel
1932—Mrs. F. S. Moody
Miss H. H. Jacobs
1933—Mrs. F. S. Moody
Miss D. E. Round
★1934—Miss D. E. Round
Miss H. H. Jacobs
1935—Mrs. F. S. Moody
Miss H. H. Jacobs
★1936—Miss H. H. Jacobs
Frau. S. Sperling
1937—Miss D. E. Round
Miss J. Jedrzeiowska
★1938—Mrs. F. S. Moody
Miss H. H. Jacobs
★1939—Miss A. Marble
Miss K. E. Stammers
★1946—Miss P. Betz
Miss L. Brough
★1947—Miss M. Osborne
Miss D. Hart
1948—Miss L. Brough
Miss D. Hart
1949—Miss L. Brough
Mrs. W. du Pont
1950—Miss L. Brough
Mrs. W. du Pont

1951—Miss D. Hart
Miss S. Fry
1952—Miss M. Connolly
Miss L. Brough
1953—Miss M. Connolly
Miss D. Hart
1954—Miss M. Connolly
Miss L. Brough
★1955—Miss L. Brough
Mrs. J. Fleitz
1956—Miss S. Fry
Miss A. Buxton
★1957—Miss A. Gibson
Miss D. R. Hard
1958—Miss A. Gibson
Miss A. Mortimer
★1959—Miss M. E. Bueno
Miss D. R. Hard
1960—Miss M. E. Bueno
Miss S. Reynolds
★1961—Miss A. Mortimer
Miss C. C. Truman
1962—Miss J. R. Susman
Mrs. V. Sukova
★1963—Miss M. Smith
Miss B. J. Moffitt
1964—Miss M. E. Bueno
Miss M. Smith
1965—Miss M. Smith
Miss M. E. Bueno
1966—Mrs. L. W. King
Miss M. E. Bueno
1967—Mrs. L. W. King
Mrs. P. F. Jones
1968—Mrs. L. W. King
Miss J. A. M. Tegart

1969—Mrs. P. F. Jones
Mrs. L. W. King
★1970—Mrs. B. M. Court
Mrs. L. W. King
1971—Miss E. F. Goolagong
Mrs. B. M. Court
1972—Mrs. L. W. King
Miss E. F. Goolagong
1973—Mrs. L. W. King
Miss C. M. Evert
1974—Miss C. M. Evert
Mrs. O. Morozova
1975—Mrs. L. W. King
Mrs. R. Cawley
★1976—Miss C. M. Evert
Mrs. R. Cawley
1977—Miss S. V. Wade
Miss B. F. Stove
1978—Miss M. Navratilova
Miss C. M. Evert
1979—Miss M. Navratilova
Mrs. J. M. Lloyd
1980—Mrs. R. Cawley
Mrs. J. M. Lloyd
1981—Mrs. J. M. Lloyd
Miss H. Mandlikova
1982—Miss M. Navratilova
Mrs. J. M. Lloyd
1983—Miss M. Navratilova
Miss A. Jaeger
1984—Miss M. Navratilova
Mrs. J. M. Lloyd
1985—Miss M. Navratilova
Mrs. J. M. Lloyd
1986—Miss M. Navratilova
Miss H. Mandlikova
1987—Miss M. Navratilova
Miss S. Graf

LADIES' DOUBLES

1913—Mrs. R. J. McNair and Miss D. P. Boothby
Mrs. A. Sterry and Mrs. Lambert Chambers
1914—Miss E. Ryan and Miss A. M. Morton
Mrs. D. R. Larcombe and Mrs. Hannam
1919—Mlle. S. Lenglen and Miss E. Ryan
Mrs. Lambert Chambers and Mrs. D. R. Larcombe
1920—Mlle. S. Lenglen and Miss E. Ryan
Mrs. Lambert Chambers and Mrs. D. R. Larcombe
1921—Mlle. S. Lenglen and Miss E. Ryan
Mrs. A. E. Beamish and Mrs. Peacock
1922—Mlle. S. Lenglen and Miss E. Ryan
Mrs. A. D. Stocks and Miss K. McKane
1923—Mlle. S. Lenglen and Miss E. Ryan
Miss J. Austin and Miss E. L. Colyer
1924—Mrs. H. Wightman and Miss H. Wills
Mrs. B. C. Covell and Miss K. McKane
1925—Mlle. S. Lenglen and Miss E. Ryan
Mrs. A. V. Bridge and Mrs. C. G. Mcllquham
1926—Miss E. Ryan and Miss M. K. Browne
Mrs. L. A. Godfree and Miss E. L. Colyer
1927—Miss H. Wills and Miss E. Ryan
Miss E. L. Heine and Mrs. Peacock
1928—Mrs. Holcroft-Watson and Miss P. Saunders
Miss E. H. Harvey and Miss E. Bennett
1929—Mrs. Holcroft-Watson and Mrs. L. R. C. Michell
Mrs. B. C. Covell and Mrs. D. C. Shepherd-Barron
1930—Mrs. F. S. Moody and Miss E. Ryan
Miss E. Cross and Miss S. Palfrey
1931—Mrs. D. C. Shepherd-Barron and Miss P. E. Mudford
Mlle. D. Metaxa and Mlle. J. Sigart
1932—Mlle. D. Metaxa and Mlle. J. Sigart
Miss E. Ryan and Miss H. H. Jacobs
1933—Mme. R. Mathieu and Miss E. Ryan
Miss F. James and Miss A. M. Yorke
1934—Mme. R. Mathieu and Miss E. Ryan
Mrs. D. Andrus and Mme. Henrotin
1935—Miss F. James and Miss K. E. Stammers
Mme. R. Mathieu and Frau. S. Sperling
1936—Miss F. James and Miss K. E. Stammers
Mrs. S. P. Fabyan and H. H. Jacobs
1937—Mme. R. Mathieu and Miss A. M. Yorke
Mrs. M. R. King and Mrs. J. B. Pittman
1938—Mrs. S. P. Fabyan and Miss A. Marble
Mme. R. Mathieu and Miss A. M. Yorke

1939—Mrs. S. P. Fabyan and Miss A. Marble
Miss H. H. Jacobs and Miss N. Richey
1946—Miss L. Brough and Miss M. Osborne
Miss P. Betz and Miss D. Hart
1947—Miss D. Hart and Mrs. P. C. Todd
Miss L. Brough and Miss M. Osborne
1948—Miss L. Brough and Mrs W. du Pont
Miss D. Hart and Mrs. P. C. Todd
1949—Miss L. Brough and Mrs. W. du Pont
Miss G. Moran and Mrs. P. C. Todd
1950—Miss L. Brough and Mrs. W. du Pont
Miss S. Fry and Miss D. Hart
1951—Miss S. Fry and Miss D. Hart
Miss L. Brough and Mrs. W. du Pont
1952—Miss S. Fry and Miss D. Hart
Miss L. Brough and Miss M. Connolly
1953—Miss S. Fry and Miss D. Hart
Miss M. Connolly and Miss J. Sampson
1954—Miss L. Brough and Mrs. W. du Pont
Miss S. Fry and Miss D. Hart
1955—Miss A. Mortimer and Miss J. A. Shilcock
Miss S. J. Bloomer and Miss P. E. Ward
1956—Miss A. Buxton and Miss A. Gibson
Miss P. Muller and Miss D. G. Seeney
1957—Miss A. Gibson and Miss D. R. Hard
Mrs. K. Hawton and Mrs. T. D. Long
1958—Miss M. E. Bueno and Miss A. Gibson
Mrs. W. du Pont and Miss M. Varner
1959—Miss J. Arth and Miss D. R. Hard
Mrs. J. G. Fleitz and Miss C. C. Truman
1960—Miss M. E. Bueno and Miss D. R. Hard
Miss S. Reynolds and Miss R. Schuurman
1961—Miss K. Hantze and Miss B. J. Moffitt
Miss J. Lehane and Miss M. Smith
1962—Miss B. J. Moffitt and Mrs. J. R. Susman
Mrs. L. E. G. Price and Miss R. Schuurman
1963—Miss M. E. Bueno and Miss D. R. Hard
Miss R. A. Ebbern and Miss M. Smith
1964—Miss M. Smith and Miss L. R. Turner
Miss B. J. Moffitt and Mrs. J. R. Susman
1965—Miss M. E. Bueno and Miss B. J. Moffitt
Miss F. Durr and Miss J. Lieffrig
1966—Miss M. E. Bueno and Miss N. Richey
Miss M. Smith and Miss J. A. M. Tegart

1967—Miss R. Casals and Mrs. L. W. King
Miss M. E. Bueno and Miss N. Richey
1968—Miss R. Casals and Mrs. L. W. King
Miss F. Durr and Mrs. P. F. Jones
1969—Miss B. M. Court and Miss J. A. M. Tegart
Miss P. S. A. Hogan and Miss M. Michel
1970—Miss R. Casals and Mrs. L. W. King
Miss F. Durr and Miss S. V. Wade
1971—Miss R. Casals and Mrs. L. W. King
Mrs. B. M. Court and Miss E. F. Goolagong
1972—Mrs. L. W. King and Miss B. F. Stove
Mrs. D. E. Dalton and Miss F. Durr
1973—Miss R. Casals and Mrs. L. W. King
Miss F. Durr and Miss B. F. Stove
1974—Miss E. F. Goolagong and Miss M. Michel
Miss H. F. Gourlay and Miss K. M. Krantzcke
1975—Miss A. K. Kiyomura and Miss K. Sawamatsu
Miss F. Durr and Miss B. F. Stove
1976—Miss C. M. Evert and Miss M. Navratilova
Mrs. L. W. King and Miss B. F. Stove
1977—Mrs. H. F. Gourlay Cawley and Miss J. C. Russell
Miss M. Navratilova and Miss B. F. Stove
1978—Mrs. G. E. Reid and Miss W. M. Turnbull
Miss M. Jausovec and Miss V. Ruzici
1979—Mrs. L. W. King and Miss M. Navratilova
Miss B. F. Stove and Miss W. M. Turnbull
1980—Miss K. Jordan and Miss A. E. Smith
Miss R. Casals and Miss W. M. Turnbull
1981—Miss M. Navratilova and Miss P. H. Shriver
Miss K. Jordan and Miss A. E. Smith
1982—Miss M. Navratilova and Miss P. H. Shriver
Miss K. Jordan and Miss A. E. Smith
1983—Miss M. Navratilova and Miss P. H. Shriver
Miss R. Casals and Miss W. M. Turnbull
1984—Miss M. Navratilova and Miss P. H. Shriver
Miss K. Jordan and Miss A. E. Smith
1985—Miss K. Jordan and Mrs. P. D. Smylie
Miss M. Navratilova and Miss P. H. Shriver
1986—Miss M. Navratilova and Miss P. H. Shriver
Miss H. Mandlikova and Miss W. M. Turnbull
1987—Miss C. Kohde-Kilsch and Miss H. Sukova
Miss B. Nagelsen and Mrs. P. D. Smylie

MAIDEN NAMES OF LADY CHAMPIONS

In the above tables the following have been recorded in both married and single identities.

Mrs. R. Cawley	Miss E. F. Goolagong	Mrs. G. W. Hillyard	Miss B. Bingley	Mrs. L. E. G. Price	Miss S. Reynolds
Mrs. Lambert Chambers	Miss D. K. Douglass	Mrs. P. F. Jones	Miss A. S. Haydon	Mrs. G. E. Reid	Miss K. Melville
Mrs. B. M. Court	Miss M. Smith	Mrs. L. W. King	Miss B. J. Moffitt	Mrs. P. D. Smylie	Miss E. M. Sayers
Mrs. B. C. Covell	Miss P. L. Howkins	Mrs. M. R. King	Miss P. E. Mudford	Frau. S. Sperling	Fraulein H. Krahwinkel
Mrs. D. E. Dalton	Miss J. A. M. Tegart	Mrs. D. R. Larcombe	Miss E. W. Thomson	Mrs. A. Sterry	Miss C. Cooper
Mrs. W. du Pont	Miss M. Osborne	Mrs. J. M. Lloyd	Miss C. M. Evert	Mrs. J. R. Susman	Miss K. Hantze
Mrs. L. A. Godfree	Miss K. McKane	Mrs. F. S. Moody	Miss H. Wills		
Mrs. H. F. Gourlay Cawley	Miss H. F. Gourlay	Mrs. O. Morozova	Miss O. Morozova		

NOTE.—For the years 1913, 1914 and 1919-1923 inclusive the above records include the "World's Championship on Grass" granted to The Lawn Tennis Association by The International Lawn Tennis Federation. This title was then abolished and commencing in 1924 they became The Official Lawn Tennis Championships recognised by The International Lawn Tennis Federation.

Prior to 1922 the holders in the Singles Events and Gentlemen's Doubles did not compete in the Championships but met the winners of these events in the Challenge Rounds.

†Challenge Round abolished: holders subsequently played through.   ★The holder did not defend the title.

THE CHAMPIONSHIP ROLL

MIXED DOUBLES

1913—Hope Crisp and Mrs. C. O. Tuckey
J. C. Parke and Mrs. D. R. Larcombe
1914—J. C. Parke and Mrs. D. R. Larcombe
A. F. Wilding and Mlle. Broquedis
1919—R. Lycett and Miss E. Ryan
A. D. Prebble and Mrs. Lambert Chambers
1920—G. L. Patterson and Mlle. S. Lenglen
R. Lycett and Miss E. Ryan
1921—R. Lycett and Miss E. Ryan
M. Woosnam and Miss P. L. Howkins
1922—P. O'Hara-Wood and Mlle. S. Lenglen
R. Lycett and Miss E. Ryan
1923—R. Lycett and Miss E. Ryan
L. S. Deane and Mrs. D. C. Shepherd-Barron
1924—J. B. Gilbert and Miss K. McKane
L. A. Godfree and Mrs. L. A. Godfree
1925—J. Borotra and Mlle. S. Lenglen
H. L. de Morpurgo and Miss E. Ryan
1926—L. A. Godfree and Mrs. L. A. Godfree
H. Kinsey and Miss M. K. Browne
1927—F. T. Hunter and Miss E. Ryan
L. A. Godfree and Mrs. L. A. Godfree
1928—P. D. B. Spence and Miss E. Ryan
J. Crawford and Miss D. Akhurst
1929—F. T. Hunter and Miss H. Wills
I. G. Collins and Miss J. Fry
1930—J. H. Crawford and Miss E. Ryan
D. Prenn and Fraulein H. Krahwinkel
1931—G. M. Lott and Mrs. L. A. Harper
I. G. Collins and Miss J. C. Ridley
1932—E. Maier and Miss E. Ryan
H. C. Hopman and Mlle. J. Sigart
1933—G. von Cramm and Fraulein H. Krahwinkel
N. G. Farquharson and Miss M. Heeley
1934—R. Miki and Miss D. E. Round
H. W. Austin and Mrs. D. C. Shepherd-Barron
1935—F. J. Perry and Miss D. E. Round
H. C. Hopman and Mrs. H. C. Hopman
1936—F. J. Perry and Miss D. E. Round
J. D. Budge and Mrs. S. P. Fabyan
1937—J. D. Budge and Miss A. Marble
Y. Petra and Mme. R. Mathieu
1938—J. D. Budge and Miss A. Marble
H. Henkel and Mrs. S. P. Fabyan

1939—R. L. Riggs and Miss A. Marble
F. H. D. Wilde and Miss N. B. Brown
1946—T. Brown and Miss L. Brough
G. E. Brown and Miss D. Bundy
1947—J. E. Bromwich and Miss L. Brough
C. F. Long and Mrs. N. M. Bolton
1948—J. E. Bromwich and Miss L.Brough
F. A. Sedgman and Miss D. Hart
1949—E. W. Sturgess and Mrs. S. P. Summers
J. E. Bromwich and Miss L. Brough
1950—E. W. Sturgess and Miss L. Brough
G. E. Brown and Mrs. P. C. Todd
1951—F. A. Sedgman and Miss D. Hart
M. G. Rose and Mrs. N. M. Bolton
1952—F. A. Sedgman and Miss D. Hart
E. Morea and Mrs. T. D. Long
1953—V. Seixas and Miss D. Hart
E. Morea and Miss S. Fry
1954—V. Seixas and Miss D. Hart
K. R. Rosewall and Miss W. du Pont
1955—V. Seixas and Miss D. Hart
E. Morea and Miss D. Hart
1956—V. Seixas and Miss S. Fry
G. Mulloy and Miss A. Gibson
1957—M. G. Rose and Miss D. R. Hard
N. A. Fraser and Miss A. Gibson
1958—R. N. Howe and Miss L. Coghlan
K. Nielsen and Miss A. Gibson
1959—R. Laver and Miss D. R. Hard
N. A. Fraser and Miss M. E. Bueno
1960—R. Laver and Miss D. R. Hard
R. N. Howe and Miss M. E. Bueno
1961—F. S. Stolle and Miss L. R. Turner
R. N. Howe and Miss E. Buding
1962—N. A. Fraser and Mrs. W. du Pont
R. D. Ralston and Miss A. S. Haydon
1963—K. N. Fletcher and Miss M. Smith
R. A. J. Hewitt and Miss D. R. Hard
1964—F. S. Stolle and Miss L. R. Turner
K. N. Fletcher and Miss M. Smith
1965—K. N. Fletcher and Miss M. Smith
A. D. Roche and Miss J. A. M. Tegart
1966—K. N. Fletcher and Miss M. Smith
R. D. Ralston and Mrs. L. W. King

1967—O. K. Davidson and Mrs. L. W. King
K. N. Fletcher and Miss M. E. Bueno
1968—K. N. Fletcher and Mrs. B. M. Court
A. Metreveli and Miss O. Morozova
1969—F. S. Stolle and Mrs. P. F. Jones
A. D. Roche and Miss J. A. M. Tegart
1970—I. Nastase and Miss R. Casals
A. Metreveli and Miss O. Morozova
1971—O. K. Davidson and Mrs. L. W. King
M. C. Riessen and Mrs. B. M. Court
1972—I. Nastase and Miss R. Casals
K. G. Warwick and Miss E. F. Goolagong
1973—O. K. Davidson and Mrs. L. W. King
R. Ramirez and Miss J. S. Newberry
1974—O. K. Davidson and Mrs. L. W. King
M. J. Farrell and Miss L. J. Charles
1975—M. C. Riessen and Mrs. B. M. Court
A. J. Stone and Miss B. F. Stove
1976—A. D. Roche and Miss F. Durr
R. L. Stockton and Miss R. Casals
1977—R. A. J. Hewitt and Miss G. R. Stevens
F. D. McMillan and Miss B. F. Stove
1978—F. D. McMillan and Miss B. F. Stove
R. O. Ruffels and Mrs. L. W. King
1979—R. A. J. Hewitt and Miss G. R. Stevens
F. D. McMillan and Miss B. F. Stove
1980—J. R. Austin and Miss T. Austin
M. R. Edmondson and Miss D. L. Fromholtz
1981—F. D. McMillan and Miss B. F. Stove
J. R. Austin and Miss T. Austin
1982—K. Curren and Miss A. E. Smith
J. M. Lloyd and Miss W. M. Turnbull
1983—J. M. Lloyd and Miss W. M. Turnbull
S. Denton and Mrs. L. W. King
1984—J. M. Lloyd and Miss W. M. Turnbull
S. Denton and Miss K. Jordan
1985—P. McNamee and Miss M. Navratilova.
J. B. Fitzgerald and Miss P. D. Smylie
1986—K. Flach and Miss K. Jordan
H. P. Guenthardt and Miss M. Navratilova
1987—M. J. Bates and Miss J. M. Durie
D. Cahill and Miss N. Provis

THE JUNIOR CHAMPIONSHIP ROLL

BOYS' SINGLES

1948—S. Stockenberg (Sweden)
1949—S. Stockenberg (Sweden)
1950—J. A. T. Horn (G.B.)
1951—J. Kupferburger (S.A.)
1952—R. K. Wilson (G.B.)
1953—W. A. Knight (G.B.)
1954—R. Krishnan (India)
1955—M. P. Hann (G.B.)
1956—R. Holmberg (U.S.A.)
1957—J. I. Tattersall (G.B.)

1958—E. Buchholz (U.S.A.)
1959—T. Lejus (U.S.S.R.)
1960—A. R. Mandelstam (S.A.)
1961—C. E. Graebner (U.S.A.)
1962—S. Matthews (G.B.)
1963—N. Kalogeropoulos (Greece)
1964—I. El Shafei (U.A.R.)
1965—V. Korotkov (U.S.S.R.)
1966—V. Korotkov (U.S.S.R.)
1967—M. Orantes (Spain)

1968—J. G. Alexander (Australia)
1969—B. Bertram (S.A.)
1970—B. Bertram (S.A.)
1971—R. Kreiss (U.S.A.)
1972—B. Borg (Sweden)
1973—W. Martin (U.S.A.)
1974—W. Martin (U.S.A.)
1975—C. J. Lewis (N.Z.)
1976—H. Guenthardt (Switzerland)
1977—V. A. Winitsky (U.S.A.)

1978—I. Lendl (Czechoslovakia)
1979—R. Krishnan (India)
1980—T. Tulasne (France)
1981—M. W. Anger (U.S.A.)
1982—P. Cash (Australia)
1983—S. Edberg (Sweden)
1984—M. Kratzmann (Australia)
1985—L. Lavalle (Mexico)
1986—E. Velez (Mexico)
1987—D. Nargisco (Italy)

BOYS' DOUBLES

1982—P. Cash and J. Frawley
1983—M. Kratzmann and S. Youl

1984—R. Brown and R. Weiss
1985—A. Moreno and J. Yzaga

1986—T. Carbonnell and P. Korda
1987—J. Stoltenberg and T. Woodbridge

GIRLS' SINGLES

1948—Miss O. Miskova (Czechoslovakia)
1949—Miss C. Mercelis (Belgium)
1950—Miss L. Cornell (G.B.)
1951—Miss L. Cornell (G.B.)
1952—Miss ten Bosch (Netherlands)
1953—Miss D. Kilian (S.A.)
1954—Miss V. A. Pitt (G.B.)
1955—Miss S. M. Armstrong (G.B.)
1956—Miss A. S. Haydon (G.B.)
1957—Miss M. Arnold (U.S.A.)

1958—Miss S. M. Moore (U.S.A.)
1959—Miss J. Cross (S.A.)
1960—Miss K. Hantze (U.S.A.)
1961—Miss G. Baksheeva (U.S.S.R.)
1962—Miss G. Baksheeva (U.S.S.R.)
1963—Miss D. M. Salfati (France)
1964—Miss P. Bartkowicz (U.S.A.)
1965—Miss O. Morozova (U.S.S.R.)
1966—Miss B. Lindstrom (Finland)
1967—Miss J. Salome (Netherlands)

1968—Miss K. Pigeon (U.S.A.)
1969—Miss K. Sawamatsu (Japan)
1970—Miss S. Walsh (U.S.A.)
1971—Miss M. Kroschina (U.S.S.R.)
1972—Miss I. Kloss (S.A.)
1973—Miss A. Kiyomura (U.S.A.)
1974—Miss M Jausovec (Yugoslavia)
1975—Miss N. Y. Chmyreva (U.S.S.R.)
1976—Miss N. Y. Chmyreva (U.S.S.R.)
1977—Miss L. Antonoplis (U.S.A.)

1978—Miss T. Austin (U.S.A.)
1979—Miss M. L. Piatek (U.S.A.)
1980—Miss D. Freeman (Australia)
1981—Miss Z. Garrison (U.S.A.)
1982—Miss C. Tanvier (France)
1983—Miss P. Paradis (France)
1984—Miss A. N. Croft (G.B.)
1985—Miss A. Holikova (Czechoslovakia)
1986—Miss N. Zvereva (U.S.S.R.)
1987—Miss N. Zvereva (U.S.S.R.)

GIRLS' DOUBLES

1982—Miss B. Herr and Miss P. Barg
1983—Miss P. Fendick and Miss P. Hy

1984—Miss C. Kuhlman and Miss S. Rehe
1985—Miss L. Field and Miss J. Thompson

1986—Miss M. Jaggard and Miss L. O'Neill
1987—Miss N. Medvedeva and Miss N. Zvereva